GW00537107

PRAISE FOR
DIRTY & DIVINE

In Dirty & Divine Alice Grist takes us on an adventure through the magical world of tarot cards. Divination comes from the Latin verb 'divinare' and literally means 'being inspired by a god'. Therefore you could say that using tarot cards is one means of putting images and words to the voices of Divine beings (or cosmic forces if you like) that offer a higher perspective on human life on Earth! As always Grist is brave, funny and very honest! You are in very good hands on this journey into mystery and you will discover the down-to-earth everyday benefits of tarot cards. I say: treat yourself to this adventure!

Imelda Almqvist, author of
Natural Born Shamans: A Spiritual Toolkit for Life
and international teacher of sacred art and shamanism

For anyone investing time, energy and passion in the journey through the tarot this is a wonderful book with a no nonsense and well grounded attitude.

I love the way Alice has so eloquently woven the tapestry of her life into the tarot to assist the reader in understanding how life situations blend with each of the tarot cards. For the beginner, this is a wonderful way of retaining the information relating to the card meanings, making it easy for them to revert back to the life situation for reference and understanding.

The book is split into manageable, easy to understand sections from the intuitive sense of the card to Alice's own journey, harnessing their power and finally the Dirty & Divine Spell-words to reinforce their meaning.

I love this book because it has such a different and unique approach to learning the tarot which is refreshing.

Joan Charles, author of *An Angel Walked Beside Me*,
creator of the Joan Charles tarot deck

Dirty & Divine brings the tarot from the esoteric, mythical, mystical, and archetypal into the blood, sweat, tears, and laughter of a woman's life. A journal-style personal walk through the tarot, this book can be used with any deck to form a unique connection with the heart of tarot... and with yourself. It reminds us of the many lessons the cards can teach us within the mundane, nitty-gritty details of daily life.

Molly Remer, author of *Womanrunes* and
Earthprayer, Birthprayer, Lifeprayer, Womanprayer

Dirty & Divine asks you to leave everything you know about tarot at the door, kick off your heels and pour yourself a cocktail.

Alice takes us through a tarot journey in a way no other tarot book has before. Forget fortune telling and learning key words, this is a real and raw look into the tarot, how it works and how it can help us understand modern life. Alice shares her own story with honesty, looking at both the shadow ('dirty') and light ('divine') sides of herself and encourages us to do the same for real transformation and even more importantly, understanding of the self. Reading Dirty & Divine was like a night in with your incredibly clever and cool best mate, getting deep and meaningful over a deck of cards and reclaiming the Goddess within, both sides of her, the dirty and divine.

New Age Hipster

Dirty & Divine isn't any ordinary tarot book... it's an invitation to meet your inner Priestess/Witch/Wise Woman. Alice's raw honesty, vulnerable sharing and feisty attitude take you on a journey, a journey through the tarot deck into your own soul! Like Alice I began 'playing' with tarot in my teens... they were dark, 'occult' and forbidden... so exciting! They also helped guide me and I used them to make huge decisions about my life. My relationship with traditional tarot cards faded as many more packs entered my life: angel cards, healing cards, runes, power animal cards even Mr Emoto's water crystal cards! I daren't count how many packs I have... three boxes full... which I now share with my women's circles. Reading Alice's book took me back to my old tarot pack, and I've started a daily journey with them. So thank you Alice, for re-igniting my tarot passion and for awakening women to their inner selves.

Rachael Hertogs, author of
***Menarche a Journey into Womanhood*, creator of Moon Times**

Alice could write about dishwashing and I'd come away from her words enlightened and inspired. Through her soul's journey into a year with the tarot in Dirty & Divine, the dishes themselves become sacred, and I am wild, wise, and ready.

S. Kelley Harrell, M. Div, author of *Teen Spirit Guide to Modern Shamanism* and *Gift of the Dreamtime*

Alice has been my go-to woman for tarot readings for years now, because her truth, knowledge + wisdom are the REAL DEAL.

In reading this book, and what Alice shares within the dirty + divine pages of it, you will have direct access to all that she knows (FYI: that's a lot), but what I find REALLY juicy about it, is that you'll experience how to use the cards + the stories, metaphors, signs + symbols they hold as a tool to help you remember your power. The fierce self-love, the courageous + wild truth of who you were before you forgot.

Let Alice, the high priestess of the tarot, take you on a journey of remembrance + reverence. The dirty + the divine.

Lisa Lister, creatrix of www.thesassyshe.com, author of *Love Your Lady Landscape* and *Witch: Unleashed. Untamed. Unapologetic*

Dirty & Divine provides a wonderful opportunity for tarot lovers and spiritual souls. Real, raw, relatable and incredibly warm. You feel as though you have a personal mentor and friend guiding you through the magic and mystery of the tarot. Alice gives fresh insight to a loved esoteric system along with real life reflections through her personal journey in her life. The addition of ways you can work with each of the cards brings a grounded understanding to the reader. Dirty & Divine is a book that will be read more than once and have a well-loved place in my sacred library.

Ethony, Tarot Goddess, creator of the Awakened Soul Oracle deck

DIRTY

&

DIVINE

a transformative journey
through tarot

Alice B. Grist

WOMANCRAFT PUBLISHING

Copyright © 2017 Alice B. Grist

All rights reserved. No part of this publication may be reproduced, distributed, or transmitted in any form or by any means, including photocopying, recording, or other electronic or mechanical methods, without the prior written permission of the publisher, except in the case of brief quotations embodied in critical reviews and certain other non-commercial uses permitted by copyright law.

Typeset and design by Lucent Word, Co. Cork, Ireland

Published by Womancraft Publishing, 2017
www.womancraftpublishing.com

ISBN: 978-1-910559-253 (Paperback)
ISBN: 978-1-910559-260 (ebook)

A percentage of Womancraft Publishing profits are invested back into the environment reforesting the tropics (via TreeSisters) and forward into the community: providing books for girls in developing countries, and affordable libraries for red tents and women's groups around the world.

Womancraft Publishing is committed to sharing powerful new women's voices, through a collaborative publishing process. We are proud to midwife this work, however the story, the experiences and the words are the author's alone.

DEDICATION

When I look to get out of myself, you pull me back in.
My people. Mab, Ivy, Clover. Keeping it real kiddos. Love you.

THANK YOU

Thank you to Lucy who saw a basic guide book on tarot, felt its seeds of something, and pushed it into a full-on destination.

With love to my Mum for showing me the spectrum and power of Womanhood, for always listening, and for being more wonderful, beautiful and inspirational than she realises. To Karen for being another mother whose divinity is in her depths of generosity.

With love to my Dad and Aileen who patiently taught an angsty teenager Tarot, who showed me a Goddess and let me make her my own. From little seedlings. . .

BEFORE YOU BEGIN

This is not a journey you need to take in isolation.
Join us at the Dirty *&* Divine private Facebook group.
Here you can discuss all that arises upon this lovely, intriguing path and share your journey with Alice and other *Dirty & Divine* devotees.

For workshops, related products and other *Dirty & Divine* guidance visit www.alicegrist.co.uk

CONTENTS

MINOR ARCANA

INTRODUCTION

OPENING THE BOX

There is something sacred within you that requires your attention. It is undulating beneath your flesh, asking you to look, pleading with you to see, to feel, to be. You might journey to Bali, take up yoga, or chant your way towards it. You could breathe deeply and determine the edges of it shifting somewhere just below your ribs. On occasion, you may feel it tickling your third eye or hear it stirring somewhere around your heart. It may pop up in the corner of your eye, in the lilt of a child's voice calling your name, in the love you make, in the strategies you employ just to survive.

There is something sacred within you, in all that you are and all that you do. In a mix of you that is everyday dirty, and spiritually divine, there is something so perfect, something more. Welcome to your journey back home; to your dirty, divine passage back to you.

This journey happens through cards. Tarot cards.

Are tarot your dirty little secret? Or divine slivers of card that you refer to when life gets difficult or decisions loom? Do you take pleasure in reading them yourself or have you preferred, until now, to keep the cards at arms' length, safely in the hands of another: a professional, a bearded lady in a booth by the sea? Or perhaps you have been curious, but too scared by their reputation, to explore tarot. Maybe this is the first time you are daring to take them into your own hands.

Wherever you are, whether beginner or seasoned tarot practitioner, *Dirty & Divine* is written for you, to accompany you on a powerful personal intuitive journey to plumb the depths of your existence and encompass the spectrum of wisdom that the cards can offer.

Take your cards into your hands, sniff them long and hard, take their scent inside. Shuffle them religiously, hold them to your heart. Ask them, as if they were the middleman to your soul, if they'd like to take a journey with you. A journey past the purposes of divination, a quest deeper than a simple spread. Ask them if they want to travel with you on a mission beyond the shallows of daily divination, a trip to unfold and reframe your life? Turn over several cards, one, two, three. . . Let these speak to you. What do the images tell you? What is your first thought, what answer or question, or adventures are illustrated? What do the cards gift to you? Are they keen? Are you?

For tarot are not just a set of cards full of lofty predictions and hope for a future husband or career. Tarot are a fast track to proper, hard-core self-knowledge and self-love. They are a tool for self-empowerment and inner understanding that is vastly misunderstood and underrated. They hold you in high esteem, recognising that you and the life you live, are worthy of sacred understanding, especially the dirty bits. In fact, it is in the dirty, filthy, human aspects, that you will find your juiciest divinity and most soulful education.

Tarot can lift you high above the grounded, earthly version of you and help you to hear the voices of ancestors, understand the spirits of the universe and maintain some personal power in a world that can be very challenging.

The power that tarot possess does not come from the cards, which are really just bits of paper with pretty pictures, but rather from the faith you learn to have in yourself as a conductor of life's magic. With tarot in your hands, and a good honest intent, faith in something 'more' and a smile on your face, you can become the Magician or High Priestess of your life. And it is from this point that this book will progress.

Dirty & Divine is a trip to your soul. It asks you to ponder and plunder your life for evidence of all that you are. The spectrum of you, from dirt accumulating under your nails, to the divine lurking in the flash of your glimmering gaze. This journey is the path of all women. The *Dirty & Divine* journey will elucidate your understanding of you, it will be an intimate illumination of life and an expansion of your world view.

All of this can be garnered from a pack of cards, should you invoke and intend it. These are kindle to your sorceress' fire as you burn through the version of self-prescribed from without, and embrace a potent stirring within. This first half of *Dirty & Divine* pokes at that, burrowing into your intent and shuffling it closer to the surface, scratching gently at the potential expansion the cards can offer.

Everything goes in this journey: you are utterly empowered to feel and experience whatever you like and to interpret it within your own realm of being. Your dirty and your divine heights and depths will be engaged in new powerful ways. We will vanquish all your constructs and get fat with self-love, sacred femininity and intuitive knowing. You will be challenged too. Don't expect this to be all angels and unicorns. It may well be hard. You may see things about yourself, about others, that you had hidden or managed to ignore. The tarot are a mirror, remember. They show utter truth. Be ready for that. Be ready for rainbows. . . and rain.

My journey as recorded within these pages, is some company for you. It keeps things real and acts as just one example. My life is that I am married, I live in middle England, I have two daughters and numerous pets. I'm an author, I read tarot, my husband is a musician. Besides our creative endeavours, we currently have day jobs. We used to be wild. Not so much these days, not so much at all. For some this may be very different to your knowing, your living. For others it may reflect your situation somewhat. It doesn't matter. You don't need to look or feel or be like me in any way whatsoever for this journey to be meaningful. My example is just one in a million. If nothing else, I hope it will help you to see your own humanity reflected through mine. Your journey, whatever that looks like, that is where your *Dirty & Divine* lies.

I have no interest in teaching you to be psychic. What I do intend is to show you how tarot are a lovely tool of your already spiritual, already intuitive, already powerful higher self. And when you connect to your higher self, the path you take will forever be changed and blessed by something higher than a pack of beautiful cardboard. You will be blessed by your own forevermore, your own illusive, etheric, cosmic, everlasting wisdom and power. What you are goes beyond words. If you could shine a light through your soul it would burst into a rhythm of sound, starlit answers, thunderous questions, arcing rainbows and a downpour of feelings. You are lightning and a bud bursting forth with blossom. That is why you are called to undertake this *Dirty & Divine* spiritual journey. So that you can marinate within it, soak alongside me and journey like a warrior fighting for her right to be what she is, to discover who she is and to spend no more time raging against what she is not and what she has become. This journey is a path back to you. Dirty you. Divine you.

OFFERING A NEW WAY INTO OURSELVES

A *Dirty & Divine* approach to tarot offers up options. It homes in on aspects of your life and challenges you to overcome them, or to make the best of them, or to continue onwards in the way you already are. It promises nothing but opportunity, potential and, when you are ready, it gives you a hotline to your own soul, your own intuition. When you have that kind of intuitive power in your backpack of life skills, you will find that the best tarot reading you ever have is the one that tells you what you kind of already know.

Let us start with this premise: all that we know of life is false. It is presented and we accept it. Yet there is more. Beyond this life. Within our essence. Under your skin. In your gut. You know this. But no words are gifted to help you explain or understand it. Religion goes some way to explain it. But religion instils fear, to keep you safe and ensure your passage to heaven. It is bastardized faith, dictated by many hands, built around greed and without the touch of a maiden, mother or crone.

Your woman's intuition has been purloined. You have been craftily removed from your own higher self, replaced by a narrower version that is pre-approved and imprinted upon the pages of any holy book. And what was originally yours — your self, your spirit — is removed, altered, made unknowable. It is transmuted into facts, behaviours and laws. Your deepest self becomes a question mark. One you are not sure you believe in.

Tarot can help lift that facade, that distance from yourself. *Dirty & Divine* shows how you can use the tarot to honour and know that complex spiritual inner self. Here you will marry up all your parts and within that find the love for you that is your most sacred gift. You will find the intuition that was always yours, that is potent.

There are many ways to get beneath the sordid shallow skin of society and break through to something deeper. Meditation is one. Yoga, maybe. Spiritual seeking is certainly another. My spiritual search always leads me back to something human. And in that humanity I discover soul. Not the other way around. Tarot are human. And they represent the gamut of all that a soul might experience in this guise. From our closest most divine self through to our filthiest, murkiest and regrettable actions. Tarot are a way to find truth.

Played well the tarot are the gateway to an alternative universe. One that was there all along, just beyond the veil, the glass ceiling, the gloss on your nails and forced smile on your lips. In playing a pack of cards between your fingers and tickling the images into your consciousness, your being, you might just infiltrate your soul and maybe, just maybe, when you find their sweet spot, you may be so lucky as to remember just who you are, deeply, dirtily, divinely.

Tarot, in my experience, stems from an inner darkness that is beautiful, cosmic and in need of expression. It answers a need of a soul trying to find answers.

Tarot addresses all of life. That is its gift. I believe tarot are well suited to any personal revolution you want to undertake, or that wishes to undertake you. Whether you aim for lofty goals, or simply want to realign with whatever is under your skin, there is much the cards can offer.

In those creatively divined slivers of paper comes recognition, and in recognition comes power. In that place of powerful self-love and truth we can glimpse our eternal spiritual selves. And once we have done that the stereotypes fall far from our understanding of self, of life, and we stand in a new rainbow of radiant light: a Goddess, a High Priestess, a King, a Queen of fucking Wands, all glimmer, haze, fire, soft edges, undefined, vanquished and yet, made more real than ever. Transformed, transforming, we become, as we always were: The Star.

Dirty & Divine will help you to draw upon the wealth of existence the cards represent, apply it to your life, and create the miracles you did not know were hiding beneath the facade of you.

DIRTY & DIVINE

So what is dirty? Other than your laundry. (Though you may feel shamefaced by that too?) You must have examples jumping to your mind. I know you do... let them arrive. Perhaps dirty is that affair you had, or wish you'd had. Maybe it is the sexuality beyond the sexuality you profess to your partner, the things you would really like to do. Dirty could be your guilt. The thing you said, the way you said it. Your truest dirt may be found in a web of lies and misgivings that you tell the world, that you tell yourself. Maybe your dirt is the grit under your nails, the art you create, and the food you prepare, full fat and astonishing. Your dirty is your humanity. It may be discovered holed up with a host of emotions: lust, greed, passion, excitement, love, hunger, fear, hate, adoration, expectation, envy, empathy... Your dirt, your filth is not the excrement of life, but the enacting of it. The things you regret, the things you most certainly don't. It is our darkness. It is that which captures you even when you try, so hard, to turn from it. It is the dark night of the soul, the questions of existence that sneak up and choke you.

Whilst divinity... well, that is something altogether other. It is the connection to a truer, higher, less-than-human self. Your divinity is purportedly unsullied: it is prayer, incense and magic. It is your connection to intuition. It is not all 'the light' though. That is a myth. It is the depth of feeling, the karma, the justice meted out against all you have felt and done. Divine is your feeling of 'something more', your inner knowing, the light at the corner of your eye, the shadow at the end of your bed. Divinity was birthing your children, or losing your mother, or finding a lost lover. It was what you learned, how it shook you, where it took you, emotionally, spiritually, transcendentally. It is the shimmer of enlightenment that raises you up and bounces off your well-intentioned words of comfort and love. Divine is unseen, harder to grasp, but you are a woman, you need not see it, you need simply feel it. Allow yourself to feel it.

Dirty & Divine are both you. That is their connection. They interface, they connect, they are the same. Yet you probably don't allow for that. You are not allowed to do that, to see that. *Dirty & Divine* are set up by a dichotomous male-led culture to be opposite poles, to keep us at odds with ourselves. If we move through this illusion though, we may be lucky to find they are the same pole, one we can straddle and spin luxuriously upon. Tarot, specifically, this journey, the *Dirty & Divine* journey, can be the wheel of fortune upon which this magical mixture starts to turn.

Dirty...

Tarot is the saviour and friend of the woman with a bit of witch in her soul, with some cheeky fairy in her step and with, no doubt, enough wonderful steaming baggage to make sense of what the cards represent. You can't come to tarot all newly scrubbed and clean. Tarot finds you, it smells your dirt out, it tunes into your bubbling, burning aura and it introduces itself. There is no turning back now. You just met your newest, most potent and yet slightly grubby best friend.

Divine...

You (we) are a little bit of stardust, a fabulous, everlasting soulful spark of energy. You are here to exist for some reason, one that you may discover, or that you may never be sure of. Irrespective of that purpose, it will lead you to encounter the ups, downs, chaos and adventure of life.

Somewhere in this mix of human meets soul is the very real fact that you are probably living in a very human way right now. This is fine, it is perfect. But I am here to remind you there is so much more: more than the version of 'human' that society demands of us. If you can wriggle a little bit out of your full-on association with being human, and embrace a little bit of your wiser, magical spirit and soul, then life can become a whole lot more spectacular.

Most of us need a little guidance and support as we get in touch with our souls. Mainstream religions have taken the tools and handed them over to the priests. Popular faith has placed a middleman smack in the middle of our relationship with the divine. We are deemed incapable and we go to God via 'his' representative on earth: the vicar, the rabbi, the guru, and oftentimes in this modern world, the yoga instructor. When you take up tarot cards you reclaim a more immediate relationship with life, with the divine, and with your own soul's journey. It is a powerful, sometimes scary, trip, but a very true, very individual route to real personal enlightenment, time and time again.

Mainstream religion and culture ask that we choose between being dirty or divine, 'good' or 'bad' — this is a false choice, as we will see, which separates us from half of ourselves. The *Dirty & Divine* approach asks that you possess and inhabit both magnificent parts of yourself. The choice you have always been offered, between the bad girl and the good girl, is a false one.

Tarot is the whole shebang. It is universal, archetypal experience and wisdom placed softly into our palms. Its illustration and symbolism unites our lost inner selves with a truly infinite, death-defying source of spiritual self. Tarot embraces our filth and our sparkle, making it real, making our hearts soar because for once something has seen our truest being.

Let me simplify. The dirty in you is not real. It is temporary. Don't sweat it. Let it be. The divine in you, that shit is real, it has guided you to this point and it does so with love. Let your dirty meet your divine and settle up somewhere midway. Keep your eyes to the skies and your feet on the ground. Give over to the craziness of it all. Throw yourself at the mercy of just how daft it can be. Feel your big feelings, then release. Let the dirt be upon you, but not a definition of you. Rise within your skin until the tingles of your vastness compute, and seek those tickles out in all that you are.

That is how it will be, in this life, and maybe the next. Here full of soul one day, lost to a plethora of stupid another. Conscious one moment, inebriated the next. You are dirty and divine and all that lays between.

TAROT AS A GATEWAY INTO MYSTERY

Tarot has taken me on a trip in my life that has saved my sanity more than once. By reading the cards and becoming immersed in their magic I started to see that there is more to life than meets the eye. Life is not just about what you can see and feel. Life is a spiritual mystery that you can start to unravel as you go through it day by day.

The tarot cards are a fabulous gateway into the mystery. Whilst you may start off a little cynical about their powers, you will soon be in awe as they throw up meaning, prediction, advice and guidance that fit perfectly for your soul. When this happens you will know that you are more than just flesh, blood and reacting synapses. You are more than a bundle of hormones, emotions, memories, pain receptors and blonde, brown, black or red hair. You are something altogether more exciting. You are the home of a powerful soul. A soul that can connect to others on deep, meaningful levels and that has a capacity for compassion, empathy and caring so profound that it blows you away, time and time again.

The magic of tarot lays not in the cards, but in how they help you to access your intuition. Whilst I love to read for others, my greatest joy comes with enabling others to read for themselves. In learning to read for yourself, you are getting to know your inner space, the spiritual self that resides underneath your oftentimes loud and overwhelming mind. The cards are a route into a more soulful life.

Tarot should never rob you of the opportunity to make your own choices. That way madness lies. If you are looking for answers or decision-making in the bottom of a teacup or amongst a set of cards, you are looking in the wrong place. The answers are always within. Always. Cards and crystal balls can reflect back your own soul. They can shine a brilliant light on your muddled mind. But as far as prediction and prophecy go I advise you to make your own, and to know wholeheartedly that it is only you who ever truly can.

The reality of tarot, is that it can offer an idea of the future, if you carry on doing what you are doing at any given time. It can't know outcomes for certain and it can only speak to your heart: it can't read your husband's mind or let you know what your teenage daughter is really doing when she comes home late. It can advise you how to react, how to change your thoughts, how to get the best out of a situation. But it can't give you details, it has no interest in gossip. Tarot when used perfectly is a signpost, a life raft and a glimpse into who you can be better.

The reality of a spiritual life is that you have free will, you can make changes, you do make changes, with every thought, feeling, interaction and deed. Of course you can mistakenly live by a plot laid out for you by a convincing gypsy casting cards on the pier. That is your choice. But in my world, tarot does not provide such black and white truths. This is not Google maps. Tarot should only ever be a map into your own heart, because what you find there is of the highest order of truth.

A regular tarot practice, for me, is more about self-help, introspection and intuitive practice than it is about anything 'psychic' or supernatural.

Tarot only reflect the reality of life. If we choose to be unrealistic about what life is, then, yes, tarot may not be the best tool for us. But I believe tarot present our options, possibilities and the truth of the life we are creating. You create your life. You can create chaos and stagnation as much as you create rebirth, beauty, love and art. The cards are simply a mirror to truth. They don't make things happen: you do. If wielded well then a pack can help guide us towards a happier, healthier, more powerfully fulfilling and abundant life.

Tarot is your guide into another side of your life as you know it. It is the dark side of your personal moon. Tarot is your buddy and your highest, wisest advisor. Tarot is you, it is you enacting your intuitive, spiritual self for the good and benefit of yourself and whomever you read for.

Tarot is magic. But many of us have been taught to be scared of magic.

TAROT, BLACK MAGIC AND THE OCCULT – SHOULD WE BE SCARED OF THE CARDS?

So is tarot of the occult? Well, yes, but only as far as the occult is a representation of self, of shadow and of dark human truth. 'Occult' is a word that frightens people — but what does it actually mean? It means 'knowledge of the hidden' — of the supernatural elements of life, which are not studied by science.

It is associated with magic, witchcraft and sorcery. All of which have been hijacked by empire-driven politics, pop culture and, of course, the veil of Hollywood. The occult has been twisted, it has been made dark, murderous, and perverse. The idea that humanity could wield such power, that women could wield such mystery, is not something that has been deemed healthy for the burgeoning realms of patriarchy. They did their best to snuff it out, or rather, burn and drown it out with the 'witches', many moons ago. Ever since then people have been scared of these practices and removed from them as forces of 'other' or of 'evil'.

Our ability to interact with the forces of nature, to turn life in our own hands, to attract and conjure and divine our paths was taken from us, blurred by a lust for commodities and conformity. Power was given to the pound and the dollar instead. They became the magic we lusted after. Money and materialism consumed us and became the wonder with which, in our hands, lives could change. Women in particular were distracted from our natural and innate intuitive wisdom by the mirror, and by all the things we could purchase to improve what we saw in that mirror. We have been distracted by ourselves. It is a clever game we have been played with. We have no miracles in our hands, but miracle cream sold to us at a high price.

The occult, particularly our natural connection with 'something more', was made 'evil', it was turned into the domain of a mythological and archetypal Satan. But the occult is not evil. I'm not even sure if evil is wholly evil, or if it is just a warped and bound up aspect of our humanity. Yet the occult remains scary because we have been told it is. It is so unknown to us. It exists outside of the life you are apportioned, outside of the cultural walls in which you are invisibly caged. It is far beyond the reach of who you thought you were. Until, perhaps, now.

Tarot cards, magic, witchery, intuition, they aren't evil, they aren't the work of the devil. Occult is just a loaded word. You can choose to change the bullet it carries. Perhaps the load that occult really encapsulates is something more powerful. Maybe, perchance, the occult, spiritual wisdom, a little witchery is our birthright? And so they call us.

Of course, some people will always feel uncomfortable with any kind of esoteric spiritual practice, especially if they have come from a strict religious background which has warned that such things are of the devil. But tarot is only as spooky as something like reading your horoscopes. Tarot comes from pagan traditions, but pagan does not mean devil. Trust me, my dad was a pagan and he is one of the nicest, most peace-loving dudes there ever was! Pagan societies worshipped nature, the earth, the mama goddesses and the father gods.

Tarot does not wield some ungodly power that causes terrible events to befall us. Tarot does not even link in with any power other than your own. Yes, some of the cards are dark and fraught with intimidating images. But life is like that, is it not? Life can be unnerving, gloomy, perverse and drenched in despair. Perhaps because of these darker cards, tarot has an undeserved reputation as being a harbinger of doom. If you pull out cards that are overly dark and dirty, do not fear. It can be unnerving to pull out the death card or the hanged man, but these have very different meanings beyond the 'obvious'. For example:

Death: Change, end of a cycle, new beginnings. I love the Death card because it means that old, outworn things are changing, making way for new life, new ideas, new situations.

The Hanged Man: Look closely at the image: he is hanging by his foot, not his neck. This card represents stasis, limbo, time to consider and to heal.

If you perform a reading that is littered with dark, frightening images you can bet your ass that you are in a dark and frightening place in your life, and the cards are simply mirroring that back at you. And the cards, being as wonderful as I know they are, will also tune into your inner genius and help suggest ways to help you feel happier, healthier and far more empowered.

Let's be really clear: tarot cards do not cause bad things, they reflect them, as they reflect all experiences of life, the light and the dark (that we often try to ignore or wish away). Tarot is a true representation of the world, and unlike angel cards that tend to be overtly positive, tarot tells it how it is: she digs into her fabulous womanly soul and commits to knowing the truth. Not a sugar-coated, fairy-wing version, but a gritty, real and raw version. As such, the darker illustrations on some of the cards allow us to tap into the pool of real dark energy that is underpinning all of our lives.

Our understanding of life or ourselves is not complete without delving the depths. You haven't seen the sea if you skim it on an ocean liner. But if you wear a wetsuit and dive, then you see it. When you get caught in a storm you feel it. When you strip naked and move from the sand to the water and swim in it, you begin to know it. Tarot is as occult as the sea is dangerous. It both is and it isn't. You are as dangerous as the sea, more so, and the occult is simply a reflection of your mysterious truth. *Dirty & Divine* escorts you past the shore, dumps the colourful plastic pedalo in the calm waters and asks you to dive.

As you flood downward into your waters you will start to recognise a self that is captured within societal walls, and another embryonic self, straining at the umbilical cord of culture. Society will take too much from you if you allow it. It takes your identity and packages it. It takes your faith and medicates it. It takes your power and placates it. It takes your fear and manipulates it. It takes your love and categorises it. It takes your instinct and educates it. It takes your soul and whitewashes her. When it has finished altering all that is base and true about you, there is little spirit left. Your heart still beats; you concern yourself with the immediate. You still feel, you still have love and hope but it is filtered through a thousand distractions and apparent needs. You become a puppet whose opinions and feelings are masterpieces of propaganda.

You are no longer yourself. Society strips us and rapes us of truth... and not just women. Anyone can be vanquished, depleted of their soul by falsehoods, appropriation of power and the assistance of institutions. Our world is one that eats itself. The cannibal few prey on the weak (those without money, without a voice, without a penis, without the correct pigment or passport). We are disenfranchised and left to play out lives fraught by convenient myth.

Tarot, in this instance, is a tool of the oppressed. It is a poignant reminder of who we can be, who we are truly. Tarot is a tool that, in itself, is just imagery. Yet those images take us in on ourselves and help to rinse the conditioning of facile institutionalized existence out of our hair. Tarot can give you back that which you did not know you had lost.

BEYOND GOOD GIRL/BAD GIRL

I've never known a 'good girl' to play with a pack of tarot.

How invested are you in seeing yourself as a good girl, or in others seeing you as one? What does being good mean to you? How do you act and feel when you take on the guise of 'good girl'?

And why are these questions important? Because many of us have been told that tarot is bad. . . and so it sets off a thrill of the forbidden in us. It dares us to take a chance on ourselves, rather than following the commandments of others. It challenges you to risk letting your bad girl out to play. It takes your good girl and your bad girl to task and ignites a rainbow of colour to unite them. It destroys the dualistic nature of being and sparks your awareness to a thousand new options, a thousand new versions of you.

And of course, good girls don't really exist. They are a far-flung fantasy of fairy tales. A good girl is as real as Prince Charming. She is a bullshit stereotype presented to a female population to make them compliant. Trying to be good has kept us trapped and small for too long. We all have a shadow side, a part of our self that we hide, that we've been taught to associate with being a 'bad girl'. We all have bad feelings and dark fantasies. All good girls are opinionated, powerful goddesses underneath the princess pink, butter-wouldn't-melt exterior, but they can get so invested in this exterior of trying to please everyone else, they become scared of their real selves, lurking under the surface. We are all dirty and divine, just some of us are more afraid of this than others to admit it and experience our fullness.

This is probably because we've been scared of being the bad girl. Bad girls, by societal rule, have tattoos, loose morals and open legs. They do what they want and not what they're told. Again, that description is reigned upon us to compound the control of the female species by forcing us to proclaim our good girl status, making us desire the traits of virginal maid, good mother, awesome wife, domestic goddess and sweet/innocent hard-done-to dumbass. Alternately we take the other route and appeal to our overlords via our tits and ass. Either way works. For someone. For him.

Such base stereotypes carry little power. Often we find ourselves swirling away from our bad/good girl facade. It is in the chaos that results from this fall whereby we uncover our inner dirt, and at the same time, if we are lucky, a pack of tarot cards show up to reflect back to us our multifaceted, good girl/bad girl, dirty/divine, whole woman truth.

Tarot offers you a powerful inlet to your actual being. Society has, of course, limited women to three stereotypes: mother, maiden and whore. All of which are heavily subjected to various states of prostitute- or slut-ridden imagery. To be accepted we must, simply must, abide in some small part to the nurturing abandon of the mama, the sweet nature of the maiden and the red lips and high heels of the slut. The subtle combination of which is tantamount to marriage material: the perfect woman.

So we squeeze ourselves into this limited variation of womanhood that doesn't bear the slightest resemblance to anything meaningful and we exist. It is a soulless place.

The tarot offers a redemptive opportunity to any woman looking for her real archetypal self. Herein we have 78 cards, all of which represent some small part of you. Some of the cards are sinful, some of the cards are powerful, some of them show strength, others orbit around your weakness, in their totality we have a spectrum of humanity. All of which abides within you.

Importantly not one of those cards is a whore or a housewife. Yes, there are maidens and mothers, but these images speak to the glorious undefined depths of those roles. Understanding this, knowing tarot, is not a textbook exercise. It is an adventure, a vision quest in reclaiming your humanity, your femininity in all its lucid and colourful depths. It is raising a middle finger to the prison of patriarchy and deciding to look inward for your vast, echoing spirit. In the modern dearth of real feminine depth, the tarot offer a true black hole — one that is warm, welcoming and transformative.

CALLING UP THE MYSTICAL WOMAN

How very convenient that something (such as tarot) which plumbs our true depths has been portrayed as something evil and to be feared. Oh, how society has abhorred a mystical woman. Oh, how we have been forced to tie down our intuitive psychic senses for fear of burning at the stake. There is no magic in our sanitised world: it is considered too occult, too scary, too Scooby Doo. Yet much like Scooby, the evil is false and lies in the hands of powerful men in masks. Unlike Scooby, the magic is real.

Any spiritual thought that empowers a person to their own divinity has been successfully driven out by institutionalised religion. Just as wars have been fought in the name of 'our' god, a more subtle attack has been waged on the inner divine. There is no money or power in connecting people to their spirit. The women, in particular, who harboured some natural esoteric longing, being so connected to their nature, to the earth, to birthing new life, were a threat. That threat was contained by the myth of domestic bliss, the longing for more 'stuff' and the hierarchy of a male science.

I do appreciate that you may not yet be comfortable with your own darkness and so you still feel unnerved. Many of us wrap up in plastic fantastic, traumas go concealed in fancy handbags and glad rags, easily denying the depths of our souls. If this is you, rather than thinking of darkness or shadow, I invite you to consider yourself to be a rainbow. You wouldn't be quite so beautiful if you took out some of the spectrum of colours.

Bad shit has happened in your life. I'm not here to 'therapise' you. But it has. And it changed you. It has added more colours to you. And it was as real as that beautiful frock you purchased that seemed to make it all seem better for, say, five minutes. All these colours are real. They may just be laying beneath the surface waiting for some recognition. In plumbing the depths of that bad shit, you do what 'the man' never wanted: you connect to self. The real self, instead of a glossed-over version. You become incredibly real in this act. Yes, that might be scary. It is easier to hide behind a glossy magazine and attend a charity event, safe in the knowing that you are good person. Yet you could know this deeper, more profoundly, and you could love yourself for it.

So, here is the hard sell: tarot is a key to the life you deserve. Rather than decorating your life with objects and adventures, this takes you inward, past your gut fauna and flora towards an internal big bang: one more intense than your best ever orgasm, and by far more lasting. Do you want an orgasm of self and do you want it to last and to bring you peace, self-love, intuition, compassion, awareness, mindful understanding of life and the people in it? Do you like the idea of being a Mystical Woman? You do? Then forget the myth that tarot is something distasteful. Embrace the bad shit along with the good, and walk towards this particular flickering light. Call her up, right now. She has been waiting patiently for you. Then shuffle and cut, ladies, shuffle and cut: your future, your self, your mystical, magical, mucky everything lies within.

TAROT –
A VITAL TOOL FOR RECLAIMING THE FEMININE

I hate to give much more of my word count to the patriarchy. Yet the divisive nature of 'woman' as it has become is beholden precisely to what a masculine world would want us to be. It's horribly simple. They aren't actually asking a lot from us. That is why the version of woman as we know it has become pretty easy to achieve: don stockings by night and an apron by day, accept a lesser paid (for the same job) role, put up, shut up, push them up and boom, you are having-it-all lass.

We have become bored. Of course we have. Rightly, we have become angry. All the hostilities that we have harboured as a result of a limiting view have spilled out across every arena, with women standing up and saying: 'No! This is not what a woman is.'

All the nasty, skewed, and oftentimes perverted, discourses raised by men, and proliferated by women, men, children, politics and the media (in public, in private, in the street and the schoolyard), are actively being challenged, right now. *Dirty & Divine* is a voice to add to this. Rather though than taking this particular version of the feminist fight to the street, or the bedroom, I am asking us to take it internally, like soul medicine.

We can be all the shades of feminine and feminist we like on any given moment and exhibit this through our placards, Twitter status and choice of newspaper. But when we curl up in bed at night, and there is no-one left to show who we really are, do we know ourselves?

Or rather do we know ourselves deeply, energetically, on a level of pure divinity and spirit? Do we know what feminine really means to us, to you? We have been fed other people's versions of it since birth, but what is your version of it? We know that we should receive equal pay, and we know why. We believe effervescently that 'No means No', and that we can do what men do. But, do we know what makes us fundamentally, femininely sacred?

Forget being equal, forget about your rights. This transcends politics and culture. Do you know why you are sacred? Do you know that you are as sacred as anybody else — penis, vagina, or otherwise?

The wise and worldly amongst us know what we are not. We are not an isolated and insipid physicality of moist vagina and welcoming, warm bosom. Those are things we may or may not have, amongst thousands of other physical attributes. They are facets of physicality and items of a corporate misogynist agenda. Much like a man is more than a tent pole in his pants and can-opening biceps. We are beyond this. So what lays beyond what we know we are not? That is the question that this journey into tarot will serve up.

Men have been lauding their 'image of god' status since time immemorial. They have truly lived the similarity. They have been the godheads, and we have been the sidekick, created as an afterthought. Their pedestal has gone higher than skyscrapers and moon landings, their empowerment has been epic, the stuff of worship. We have equalled all else that men are, *Dirty & Divine* helps us equal that 'other' hot potato. It gives us the goddess within. Matching their god. Being our own unique, personal version of sacred.

I believe the tarot can provide an answer and carry us deeply into a version of feminine. It shoos us past the wispy allocations of youth, the morose repetitions of middle age and it finds us open and expansive in some ageless, un-earthy space. Herein we uncover a version of self so unique and empowering that it perversely alters for every woman who attends this journey.

There is no recipe for woman, but a million shades and pitches, with thousands of octaves and colours occupying each one body. We are complex and crystalline, dirty and divine. . . and that's all just words. It's just letters formed to make you think a certain way. We are moving beyond the alphabet here, beyond the walls and structures of words. Words are but a prison that render divinity defunct. *Dirty & Divine* ushers you into the sacrosanct space of self that only you, on some cosmic, genome level, fully understand.

Dirty & Divine gifts you the chance to use the tarot to open to the greatest you that currently sits unfathomed beneath the distractions of the flesh, the mind games of society and the facades of consumerism. Life is yours to toy with. The world around you is mythical and based upon the world views of the very few. You have lost all power. You never really had it, you have been raised powerless. Perhaps you regain some power through love, through parenting, through career and payments. None of these things are real. None of them are permanent. Life is deceptive like that. The things we are told are false, are in fact the things which are most true. And these things, these facets, these subtle winds that wake you in the night and leave you wanting something more, but unsure of what, these are your true powers. They want you to grasp them, use them and in return they will make you whole.

It is time to leave the safe comfort of the life that has been painted for you, and to begin to mix your colours with your own hand. Begin with the premise that you are everything, and everything you have been taught as normality is nothing. Trust that all that arises as you move towards the tarot journey is a giant orgasm of self, rushing through to sweep you into a place of immense self-knowing, inevitable self-love and undeniable intuition. It sounds powerful, because it is.

There is no reason to do this *Dirty & Divine* journey. Place feminism, spirituality and self-help aside. It is a benefit of living in a still selectively free world. And should you choose to use that vote, to elect to be yourself free from constraints, then this is a way to go. Not THE way. Just a way. A powerful, permissive, engaging way.

We are all looking for answers and how to live in a world turned upside down. For women in this current climate, these cards can help to consolidate all that you are. They can expose the best of your existence. Used wisely they can heighten your senses and enlarge your self-knowing. They take the culturally thin myth of what it is to be female, in your skin, and they kindle it into something substantial. They add muscle and meat, soul and simmering. They take your good girl and they raise it, sully it and engage something deeper: your shadow, your non-logical intuitive wisdom.

This book is written particularly for women. And for those who wish to access their innate femininity, regardless of physicality. Femininity, femaleness, girliness and being woman are all things that until recently have been deprived of weight. Both literally and metaphorically. To be a woman was to be less than. It still is. I believe there is a resurgence of womanliness afoot. Feminism has risen from its early ashes and is infiltrating all things. No longer does it come under one solid hashtag, but under a myriad of guises. In all things that women touch, a little revolution is taking place. For me, the mystic, the cosmic, the spirit and the tarot, is my little slice of that action.

The call to tarot is one that goes deeper than our everyday self. There is a raging desire on behalf of cast out femininity to embrace all that we have lost. There is a feminist element in skewing and expanding upon what 'woman' has become. It starts with you and it blows out across sisters, mothers, daughters and generations above and beyond. We owe a full spectrum of self to the past, and the future.

Now, with all this talk of women and the feminine, please don't think this book is inherently sexist. Whoever you are, gender being somewhat irrespective, this book is written to help you recognize yourself, to become at one with your dirty, your divine, and the spectrum that lies between and beyond.

If you happen to be a guy, then congratulations on accessing your inner feminine. For, in my mind, any dude playing with a pack of tarot is essentially in touch with his deeper, feminine assets, at least a little. And that is how it should be. For too long men have spurned the little bit of goddess within their soul for a prolonged and concerted effort to be 'all man'. Yet tarot, when understood deeply, requires us to open to a rainbow of identity:

man, woman, animal, plant, other. So if you are a dude, sullied up with life, wielding a pack, ready to be more than your male limitations, then welcome. Let's marry up our High Priestess with your Magician and get this *Dirty & Divine* journey on.

MY RELATIONSHIP WITH TAROT

Tarot have mustered a love affair with myself, with my many facets and deep mysterious knowings. They have shown me that I know things I could never have known. And I trust that this is because I am something more beautiful and wonderful than the flesh I sit in.

I was fourteen years old when I purchased my first ever pack: Astrotarot by Russell Grant. Since then a pack of cards has never been far from my side. My initial use of tarot cards, was, of course, consumed wholly with what they could tell me about my love life. When my Wiccan dad and stepmum would read for me, all I was waiting for was the card that told me that true love was coming. Alright, forget true love, really I just wanted a nice boyfriend, a bit of a snog. Like many teenagers before me, the world revolved around me and my desires, and so for some time, that is how I used the cards, as prophesier of how likely or not I was to get hooked up. For years and years those cards were barren on the boyfriend front. It was frustrating. But it reflected truth. Compared to many of my school friends I was a late starter.

But then I got started... My favourite tarot memory occurred somewhere amidst the melee that was losing my virginity, getting stoned and drinking far too much. I was staying at my friend Jenny's house whilst her parents were on holiday. This was our very own American-style crazy spring break. We were seventeen and a little wild. We had friends round every day, parties every night, we drank illegally, and possibly smoked a bit of weed and I finally hooked up with a dude. As stated this was an important two weeks: Jenny got herself a long-term boyfriend and I lost my virginity to the guy who I had harboured a crush on since, like, forever. It was a rites of passage fortnight, but one soaked in modern terms, sex, drugs, rock and roll, oh, and a little bit of tarot too.

The stand out memory I have of that two weeks was not the obvious one. It was not the memory of popping my cherry, that was, in fact, rather forgettable. It was not my shamanic weed-induced feeling that the grass in the garden could feel pain. It was instead the mega tarot session that I performed for around twenty young folks who literally lined up around the side of the house for their cards to be read. These teenagers, surely, had better things to be doing, like partying and fucking. Instead the word spread and before I knew it I had a captive audience who were willing to forego the dancing, drinking and youthful fumbling and who instead submitted themselves to something a little bit spiritual.

I loved every second of those readings. They taught me something, too. They taught me that beyond the laddish bravado, the drunken banter, the girls' thick make-up, we are all sweet little souls, stumbling through life, looking for something a little bit deeper to grab onto. My tarot cards were a life raft that night, they taught me about people, and they taught people a little something of their soul beyond the teenage culture of instant fulfilment. I have never felt prouder, as person after person marvelled at how I knew them, at how I had read their lives and how the advice I gave was just perfect. What an unexpected privilege.

This was a turning point. With my virginity a distant memory, my use of the cards shifted. No longer was I so concerned with that particular milestone, and instead I began to use the cards as a tool to spiritually activate and intrigue other people. At the same time, my use of tarot meant I was connecting with some fundamental universal archetypes and understandings of life. Some people take a lifetime (or several) to uncover such truths. Yet the cards afforded me a glimpse into a human spiritual condition often unfamiliar to one so young.

When I was a youth, tarot felt all-powerful. In honing my tarot skills, I felt I had an ability to connect with others. This ability was like an icebreaker in any situation. I was a shy kid really, yet with tarot cards in my hand I could talk to people on the deepest possible level. I could uncover their soul and see past all the devices and delusions that they surround themselves with, and I could see them, the true them in all their colours and dimensions. It was a beautiful experience, and one that I treasured.

I have learned over time, and with the inevitable maturing benefits of age that tarot cards are not necessarily a great party game. That special night my readings were treated with reverence and respect. These days I take my tarot with green tea and homemade cupcakes and would not recommend conducting sessions whilst under the influence of anything. But to be real, to keep my story honest, I will confess that my early tarot learning was set amongst the paraphernalia of youth, and, yes, that meant parties and craziness.

The beginning of my tarot journey also marked the end, for a while. The transcendental nature of youth and living for the weekend, proved to be a superior option to a pack of cards. Quite rightly. From the age of 17 to 27 my card use was minimal and mostly private. My energy went elsewhere, to living, to being young, to being bad and indulging behaviours that mainly made me feel shitty.

My energies, my spiritual energies were sapped by my focus on the weekend and the substances that made the weekend seem so fabulous and the week so goddamned dreary. This went on until around the age of 28 when I was drawn towards my soul again. Here, and with more experience under my belt, I started to truly prepare for adulthood, for motherhood, and for hanging up my wilder tendencies for good. In this change the cards came out again. As the drunken nights became fewer the next ten years have been devoted to spirituality, birthing life and starting to understand myself more deeply. The rebirth of me that kick-started just before my Saturn return has seen my use of tarot return too. I have honed my craft and my readings have become imbued with unconditional love and cosmic universal awe. My reading are no longer about impressing a bunch of boys in a kitchen, but about guiding folks through the tumult that is life. And if I kick-start a few wandering spirits towards their soul and towards their intuition then my work here is done.

As I've grown into my understanding of tarot, I see them now as a good friend. One who is willing to impart fabulous, soulful, friendly advice to anyone who'd like to hear what they have to say. Whilst tarot started out about my experience of other people, they have morphed into a roadmap to my own inner self. Through them I get to know my personal intuition and my soul. Tarot are a tool for self-empowerment and inner understanding like nothing I have previously known before or since... and I have done my fair share of spiritual explorations.

This *Dirty & Divine* journey is the next step for my personal tarot journey. The aim is to help me better understand myself and to take my tarot knowledge deeper. I intend for it to forage the fodder of my soul and to reveal who I am, who I can be and what I should know right now. I am placing a call via my tarot deck to the sacred feminine. Her answer, I believe, will be exhilarating.

The thoughts, coincidences and events conjured through this journey will provide a glimpse of a mystical self that is intoxicating. I hope to engage new parts of my higher me, but also parts of my human self that have been buried deep beneath a cardboard cut-out of 'woman', one whose shadow has eclipsed me for far too long.

As her thin shadow retreats something super ascends. From my grubby, burdened flesh arises a Witch, a Warrior, a Priestess, an Empress, a Queen and, yes, a Princess. Not to mention the Lover in my heart, the Star in my reflection, the Hermit in my wondering. Where have they been, and why was the cardboard woman so compelling? How did she so effectively bury the archetypes that are forgotten in my flesh, in yours?

Enough of me. This is your journey to undertake. It is a quest of shedding the known and embracing the (almost) forgotten. Because these tarot archetypes, the women depicted within them and the versions of you they reflect, never left you. They raised up when you needed them, roaring, witty, loving and bold. Then they tucked back down to the bottom of your high-heeled shoe, trampled on and pedicured into nothing but a flash of a memory.

This *Dirty & Divine* quest is one that calls upon those quashed parts to raise up and form a deliriously enchanting part of your everyday self. The path you take will forever be changed, blissed out and blessed by something higher than a pack of beautiful cardboard. Blessed by your own forevermore, your illusive, etheric, cosmic, everlasting wisdom and power. The cards are nothing but a spade and shovel to uncover the spirit inside you, your feminine divine.

Let us begin digging.

THE JOURNEY

JOURNEYING THE CARDS

I have lived the cards for 25 years. I have learned the cards through thousands of readings for friends, clients and myself. I have drawn a card for myself most days over 25 years. Sometimes several times a day, dependent on life circumstances.

Most books will teach you variations on spreads and various theoretical meanings. But my intention for this book is to bring the cards alive. To begin with I toyed with writing a standard section detailing the meaning of each and every card. But I became so horribly bored with that, so instead I opened to something else. I was sent the inspiration that this second part must be a journey, your journey, one where I lead and you follow. So instead of harping on about some official card meanings, we live life through the lens of each card, for 78 days, and we make it real, gritty and personal.

Yes, that's right, we bring the tarot cards to life. We bring them into our lives.

I loved the idea in theory, and it was quite tempting just to keep it as a safe tidy idea, but to know the power of this approach, first I had to do it myself. I had to let the cards out of their box and into the chaos and mundanity of daily life.

Before writing this book I had never journeyed the cards. I had never handed over my life to a card, per day, or per week, and asked it to do what it wanted with my world. I had never gotten quite that intimate. So how could I ask you to do so, when I hadn't got past third base? I had never lived the cards.

So rather than ramble on about what you should do to connect to the cards in a hypothetical way, I'm just going to do it. Goddess only knows what personal insight this might bring up. But I hope that as I live it, and you read it, we can get acquainted on whole new levels, with the imagery, with each other, with ourselves.

HOW TO USE DIRTY & DIVINE

Here is how I recommend you use this journey.

Firstly, you must find the right pack of cards for this quest. Perhaps you already own them, maybe you need to go shopping. We each have a strong emotional/soul/aesthetic pull to certain cards, and others leave us cold. Bearing in mind you're going to be spending a lot of time with these cards, it's best to pick a pack that make you curious, excited, intrigued. Take some time to choose your pack — there are hundreds if not thousands out there. Allow your intuition to guide you as you pick, allow the cards to speak to you.

Cards are available online, or in your local New Age store. I personally used the Spiral deck to undertake my journey. There are so many to choose from: traditional, angelic, gothic, artistic, funky and punky. When you find the right pack, you will know. If some of the images challenge you, plough onwards. There are certain cards that I still struggle with, and I found, in my journey, these held the most intriguing insight.

Once the right cards are in your hands, you are ready to begin. The first time you do this journey (and I hope you will do it many times over the years of your life), you would be best placed to start from the first card, The Fool, and follow through in the order I have set out (perhaps jumping back and forth a little if you feel that fits your journey). You may also, if you wish, and if you feel called to, choose to shuffle the cards and take a new one at random every day until you have worked through the whole pack. Either way works. Be guided by your intuition and follow the path you feel is yours.

As you journey the day with each card, allow yourself to flow into it, and it into you. Try not to have expectations around what each day will bring, because it is not as obvious as it seems.

My journey acts as a little illumination, an example of what happened to me, what thoughts rose up as my day unfolded and what events befell me as the cards took hold. Please don't expect your path to even remotely echo mine: it may do, it may not. You do not need to be like me in any way. The details of our lives may be similar or far flung from one another. I am just one example of how tarot can dance and play out upon a life. Your task is not to emulate my journey, but simply to be inspired by my soul-seeking. Allow my journey to reverberate around you and then slip away as the events of your day, your life, your living, unfold.

You may wish to read my journey section before you enact your day with the card, perhaps the night before. Or, it may be that you read it afterward, after your day's adventure is complete. You may also like to read the whole book before starting your journey, and then reference it as and when you like. Again, and I can't stress this enough, go with your intuition, the way you feel: this is the way that will work for you.

It is important that you keep a diary of each day. I often didn't realise what I had learned until I started writing. Wisdom would flow from me when I hadn't known it was even there. On days when I thought nothing much had occurred, my inner world was alight with thought and concept, that only properly took hold when placed upon paper. So be the reader, but most importantly, be the writer: allow your experience to become a true, real thing, commit it to ink and write your own *Dirty & Divine* book.

Meditate, gaze at each card and assimilate it into your day, carry it with you for reference, or sleep with it under your pillow. Bring its message forward and allow it to become entrenched in all that you do. Understand that by the end of the path you will be quite changed, challenged and wonderfully enlightened. This isn't just about tarot; this is full on soul-seeking.

Each day in this *Dirty & Divine* tarot journey is divided into

'Intuitive Meaning', 'My Journey', 'Harness the Power of...'
and a 'Dirty & Divine Spellword' sections. The intuitive meaning
gives an overarching meaning that reflects the 'official' meaning
but also my gut feeling on it. Yours may differ. And that matters.
If your intuitive meaning screams something different to mine.
Cool. Be with this. Make each card your own, make your
understanding be the one you defer to, every time.

The Dirty & Divine Spellword is gleaned from the bowels of my
path. Use it as a heads up. Then again, discard it and create your
own. Use it as a rocket ship to launch your day, or sink it and
envisage something different.

As you move past the Major Arcana, and into the Minor suits,
the details may become trickier, the events (may be) subtler, the
meaning of the cards may seem more elusive. There are many
ways to expand your understanding of the card, and to inform
your day as you continue onward. Feel free to Google the hell
out of card meanings, and then take what you learn and twist it
around your curves. Make it your own. Every damn day. Make
that card about you. Own the journey.

A BRIEF INTRODUCTION TO THE CARDS

Before we start our journey, I just want to give those of you
who are just beginning your tarot adventure a brief overview of
the cards.

The 78 cards of the tarot are divided into the Major and
Minor Arcana.

The Major Arcana are numbered 0 to 21 and represent strong
themes, characteristics, archetypes, people and situations. If these
cards come out in a spread, then they reflect a major or important
element of your life. The images are powerful and will likely carry
a potent message for you. The Major Arcana taps into archetypes
of humanity, so in here you will find characters that reflect the
essential beings in our society: mother, father, priest, lover, devil.

You will very likely know a person who fits each card, you will see aspects of yourself in some or many, or even all of them. The 22 Major Arcana are what makes up the soul of humanity. They decorate every room, every home, every town, every café, every beach, every war zone and every hospital of this planet we call Earth.

The Minor Arcana are divided into four suits: Swords, Wands/Batons, Cups and Pentacles/Coins. They are numbered Ace to Ten and each suit has four court cards: Knave/Page/Princess, Knight, Queen and King. These 'minor' cards tend to capture the subtleties of life. They don't speak so loudly of the human condition as the Major Arcana, but they seize and reflect the daily grit that we all must address throughout our lives.

The Minor Arcana are themed into different areas of life, which certainly help when trying to distinguish a card's meaning. The themes of the suits are:

Swords — AIR — Sword themes include: thought, information, connection, ideals and self-expression.

Wands/Batons — FIRE — intuition, vision, progress, individuality and failure/success.

Pentacles/Coins — EARTH — senses, materialism, external reality, finances, work and tangible humanity.

Cups — WATER — deep emotion, love, fear, sorrow, the learnings and depths of relationships.

THE JOURNEY BEGINS

Dirty & Divine tarot is all about tapping the often unexplored resource that is your spiritual self. You may believe that this spiritual self is helped along by a host of angels, guides, cosmic, loving energies. That's fine. You are probably right.

But in the beginning I advise you to simply look deeply at the image and allow it to speak for itself. I've said it before, and

I will say it a million times more, your impression and feeling of a card, is the right interpretation. This is an acquired skill, trusting yourself, but it is one you can absolutely embrace and learn. What does the colour of the card mean to you? How does the image make you feel? Do any words or memories spring to mind? Does the person on the card remind you of anyone? Put your music onto shuffle and as you look at each card, see what is playing. Let the radio flow in the background and reverberate around you. Draw cards in the bath, in bed, in a garden, by a lake, in the toilets at work, in the car and by the sea. On a very basic level consider this: does each card make you feel good or bad, or perhaps confused and indifferent?

As you gaze upon and start to connect to each card you must simultaneously learn to quieten the big loud voice in your head that knows better than everyone else. This voice can do damage. This voice can over-speak your honest intuition. Your heart whispers that a card is joyful, your head might shout that it is arrogant or unrealistic. Place the big head thoughts to the side. Listen to the soul-speak that bubbles up softly and subtly.

This isn't easy. The very act of practicing tarot is a way to help quieten that loud voice, and it may take months or years or even decades to perfect. This *Dirty & Divine* journey is one way to learn how to access your intuitive spiritual nature. The knock-on effects in your life will be incredible. Because as you journey each card, you will learn to give over to a flow of higher spiritual wisdom.

This wisdom doesn't stop when you put the cards away. If you want it to it can become a beautiful part of your existence, forever. That higher spiritual wisdom, is, after all, you. It just happens to be a part of you that you don't use very often at the moment. But, like an unexercised muscle, it will get bigger, more defined and powerful the more you trust it and flex it. Simply opening yourself to the possibility of that spiritual muscle is the first step towards a divinely aligned life.

You may find that you want to marry up your understanding of the cards with other modes of divination. Whatever helps inform your understanding is perfectly acceptable. Accentuate your journey by supplementing it with any of the following. Angel/guidance cards. Numerology. Astrology. Daily horoscopes. Spiritual practice and learning of any kind. Crystals. Runes. Vision Boarding. Surfing. Yoga. Meditation. Juicing. Dance. Art. Feng shui. Healing. Reiki. Pilgrimage. Flower Remedies. Prayer. Tarot combine nicely with many other soulful and wellbeing modalities. Power up however you see fit.

My final word, as we begin, is this: you have total freedom to take this journey as it meets you. The key to understanding tarot is the ability to accept what arises within you when you look at any card. You are the key. You are the interpreter. My writings and interpretations are but a bit of whispered inspiration. You are the wise woman of your life. I am not your High Priestess. You are. The real clues to what any card means to you, lays in the whispering of your heart, the images that spring to mind, the events that befall you. Let your life, your heart, your soul, lead. Trust that you are right, every time. You are right. Now to begin. . .

MAJOR ARCANA

We begin with the Major Arcana, the home of archetypal power. These are big cards that span the gamut of humanity. Herein we have the whole rat race, the whole angelic host of all that you are. Each card reflects a slice of yourself, people you have known, who you would like to be, and who you would not. Beyond this they are themes of life: war, peace, love, hate, pride and failure. All of this is encapsulated within the universe that is you. Tarot has a lovely way of pulling it out, showing it to you, making you observe your humanity. Yet the knowing, the inner understanding we can garner if we open our eyes to all that we are, well, that really is something special.

I will say no more, because what happens next, is your journey. Your sacred tarot journey.

0 – THE FOOL

INTUITIVE MEANING

The Fool speaks from your intuition as a call to freedom. Not the freedom of nothingness, but the freedom of heading towards your goal, and, to an extent, saying 'sod it' to the consequences. The Fool asks you to dig into a youthful exuberance, one that is unmarred by bad experience and to trust the journey. That journey may not always be smooth, it may sometimes be difficult or chaotic, but there is love and compassion within this. We are born to experience life, in all its craziness and wonder. The most potent way to do this is with faith that everything that occurs is 1) created by us, through our thoughts, feelings and deeds and 2) all-perfect, even the seemingly imperfect. The Fool asks you to have faith in the path you have chosen, to know you can change it if you wish, and that the key to doing so lies in self-knowledge, trust and heading joyfully and positively into every moment.

MY JOURNEY

The foolishness of my task was apparent when I at first could not locate The Fool card in my pack. Having whipped through the set, I was perplexed as to its whereabouts. I glanced down and there he was, poking out from the pile. A portender that attention to detail may be important over the next 78 days.

I stared hard at the card. Something I have not done in a while. When one becomes familiar with a thing, one tends to stop seeing. This goes for all things. I wasn't expecting much because I know the card. It has a well-thumbed page in my mind that I refer to regularly. But the lengthy gazing soon gave way to some intriguing thoughts.

I started off thinking about the crows that adorn the card. Then I was drawn to the glowing chalice and this divine memo arose in my mind. . .

You think you know what you are looking for. In foolishness towards that quest and its outcome you are guided forward. Your inclinations are bent to a spiritual will as you seek onward. And what you seek is something altogether different from what you tell yourself today. Something better and altogether more wonderful. Yet you won't know it till you reach it, and you can't attend to it without stumbling forward towards something, anything. So head towards the glow up ahead, tell yourself whatever you need to get your feet moving. Know that what you want, what you need, and what is truly yours to be had are beautifully different from the myth your mind believes.

I wasn't expecting that. Though it makes all the sense in the world. The fog of humanity blurs our heart's destination, our sight. All we can do is move through the ether towards a little something. It's not even 9am yet. The Fool has spoken. I am opening to more wisdom today. Crack out your Fool card (if you can find it) and let's start strolling towards the glow.

The Fool's journey is arduous and easy: pay attention, live in the moment and things flow. Fight the flow and life gets hard. There is a degree of invocation within this. We call upon what we think we need, and that leads us towards what we really require. Our journeys are full of foolishness, that is their totality. Yet within the foolishness, the chaos, the unexpected swerves, we find wisdom. As we live we hang on less to outcomes, and yet the Fool will still urge us forward to trip us up. Other days he guides us gracefully towards all that is, but it is up to us not to get distracted along the way by something shiny. From here we stumble towards our own greatness in whatever form it unexpectedly arises.

What more can we do? We must hear our Fool's call and move towards her gold, her goal. What comes of this is irrelevant. The journey will show us what we need.

HARNESS THE POWER OF THE FOOL

Push beyond your comfort zone on any one small thing, every, single day. Eat differently, meet up with that friend, make that call, catch a bus or walk instead of driving, go into that restaurant that slightly intimidates you. There are so many simple ways we can embrace the bravery and bravado of The Fool.

Keep a note in your *Dirty & Divine* tarot journal of how breaking out of your comfort zone makes you feel. Then go ahead and break it some more.

DIRTY & DIVINE SPELLWORDS OF THE FOOL

I charge ahead without fear, I am protected by my trust, faith and willingness to learn.

1 – THE MAGICIAN

INTUITIVE MEANING

The Magician calls you to connect your spirit to the universal energies that flood through your veins. This card speaks to your ability to utterly manipulate your world, to create wonder, from the inside out, not the outside in. He asks you to find the magic in your soul and when you do, to bring it outward and to share the beauty of faith, spirit and belief with others.

The Magician has the ability to take the most meagre of ingredients and craft a miracle. Your life is as you choose to create it, and any thoughts of lacking control, are nothing but false modesty hiding your true potential. You are a wonderful spark of soul, your thoughts create your existence and you have the power within you to make change happen. Trust in your own power. Step forward with faith. Consider the life you want and then walk towards it with full inner knowing. Now is the time to embrace your inner Magician, the all-powerful Witch in your soul, mix up a potion and make things happen!

MY JOURNEY

I've always struggled with this card. He has struck me as a devious, dubious kind of chap. One who plays with smoke and mirrors. I have felt, though, that my understanding of such a powerful archetype is far too limited. I have drawn myself away from deeper consideration of this card because it makes me uncomfortable. I don't quite get it, and I don't like that. So a whole day with it as my guide felt ominous.

It wasn't an ordinary day either, it was a day of burying a friend who died too soon. Whilst this was remarkable, that which came with it was not so. It was a typical day one might associate with a funeral. We got ready, I wore black, people cried, it was moving.

Within the day there were inevitable moments that might be chalked up to The Magician. The funeral we attended was late because the hearse forgot to pick up the family. We had a long wait. At one point a horse-drawn carriage bearing the hearse of a baby rounded the corner. Holding my own baby of only four months old in my arms, I was moved deeply. I walked away to give the family some respite from my healthy bouncing and loudly crying baby. As I did so I was assaulted by graves bearing the name of my first born. I didn't take this as an omen. But as a reminder of life being short. And yet we are under the illusion of longevity, influence and purpose.

That funeral helped me remember that the only real purpose is to love and be loved. Any ambition beyond that is sand to the wind. Here I find the meaning of The Magician: life is illusion. No wonder this card has always made me struggle, made me want to shuffle past it quickly and bring forth something more readily adaptable to that illusion.

We are all conspiring with that illusion, sometimes happily, sometimes with misery, for some it is too hard, whilst others manipulate that illusion to their whim. And it all seems so unfair. Yet the power to shift that illusion towards our foolish journey is simply a matter of understanding life differently, understanding that illusion and waving your wand over it.

Digging deep for themes such as love and happiness, will take us on a different journey through the illusion to something that exists beyond it: to consciousness, to our spirit, to our most magical self. And whilst certain illusions can add to our abundance and therefore effectively raise our happiness, temporarily (oh how I'd love to make my millions), it's no guarantee of anything. Love though, happiness though. . . think on that.

I'll be honest, when I finished the day of The Magician, I wasn't convinced I'd learned anything. Then I took to this page and it all poured forth. I advise you to write your journey religiously, or speak it to a like-minded friend. Make sure you process it, because objectivity and understanding is gained through that.

And finally I'd like to share a little obvious magic that did occur on my Magician's journey. Later that night, girls tucked up in bed, my husband and I were chatting about the matters of success, money and the like. He had been advised by a friend at the funeral that he can manifest money… and wouldn't he like to make lots of money? My husband, in his sweetness, shut the conversation down by remarking that no, that didn't matter to him, that all he wanted to be was happy. At this point of our chat my husband's phone, sitting untouched on the side, piped up with a female voice, 'That sounds good to me!' she chirped. And whilst I can't claim to definitively see through all illusion, I am pretty certain that money is an illusion of the highest order, and therefore, the idea of seeking only happiness, sounded pretty good to me too. It is remarkable how a chink can appear in the matrix and guide us forward. So, to whoever or whatever magician took control of my husband's phone to give us that auditory high five, I thank them.

HARNESS THE POWER OF THE MAGICIAN

Get magical, invoke wonderful things, call upon your angels and guides and ask for assistance. Don't sit waiting, but do trust that it will come in unexpected ways. Imagine yourself to be a magnet attracting all that you truly need.

Cast a spell — don't look to ancient wisdom or the spells section of your fave glossy soul magazine, instead, invent your own. I do this all the time. A few candles, some powerful words, some longing intent, some fire to burn or earth to bury, some stars to wish upon, a moon upon which to focus. Use any or all of that in whatever order suits. Invoke angels, guides, goddesses, ancestors or your much-loved and missed friend/grandma/auntie. Call upon the spirit of the wind or your beloved pet dog. Spells are simply a testament of desire and trust. The first place to enter into trust, is in understanding that you are a purveyor of magic. So purvey away.

DIRTY & DIVINE SPELLWORDS OF THE MAGICIAN

I am raw magic. I allow it to infuse me and create miracles.

2 — THE HIGH PRIESTESS

INTUITIVE MEANING

The Divine Feminine resides here. The High Priestess is feminine spirit, the higher self of woman. She stands in antithesis of all the masculine godheads. Her connection to the magic of nature has been snuffed out. Her role replaced by middlemen, priests, scriptures, books and rules. Her being is the power of humanity to connect to their spirited selves. She is the messenger and vessel of a one-to-one relationship with divinity.

The High Priestess is the female leader of the past: the wise woman, the sage, the priestess on the mount that folk revered and held in great esteem. She soothes souls, she anoints life, she brings forth an ancient power. She is light and dark, earth and sky, fire and water. She connects to the unseen, to the 'something more', and she brings it to life.

The High Priestess teaches you that you are your own goddess. You are linked to all things divine and you can channel that wisdom through your soul, your heart and your intuition. Dip into your inner knowing. Listen closely to your heart's whisperings. Trust that you have the power to create your life from within. Get witchy, cast a spell, invoke something wonderful. There is great wisdom within you, allow it to come out to play. Make the world your own. Birth it from your soul.

MY JOURNEY

I'm excited. All of the previous insight regarding The Magician came on the day of The High Priestess. She is the most powerful interpreter. She takes the silence of the male, and issues it with meaning. She comes to understand the world through the periscope of her incredible intuition and insight.

If I'm having an arrogant moment, I like to align myself as her. She is my witchy soul; she is our wisest stepmomma. She is the depth and power and magic I'd love to see in myself. It's still morning, I have a day of tarot readings ahead, so I hope her energy bodes well. Ms Priestess, I am your willing daughter, let's do this.

The High Priestess certainly visited today, but I am so accustomed to her energy that it's hard to decipher any one thing. I had two tarot clients, our session was special and I recognised that they both had High Priestess hearts. Which was lovely. We had a little coven going for a few hours and put their lives to rights. Their inner Priestesses came to the party and they did some incredible soul searching, realising and connecting to self.

That is one thing about The High Priestess: she is very personal. My High Priestess can't tell yours what to do. She must arise within an individual and take that soul deeper within their own being. She isn't there to overwhelm or direct others. She attracts and manifests her own existence: her own magic is her adventure, her divinity is her desire and her accomplishment. She is her own mother, nurturing her soulful nuances in quiet, powerful ways. She doesn't change the world, she changes her world, and whatever knock-on effect that has, so be it. She has boundless faith and utter trust. She feels her own inner layers and meticulously peels them back.

I felt good today. I felt in control of myself, my being, my interactions, my magic. I was aware. Conscious. Composed, confident and at ease. It was lovely. I glided through the day, full of myself, or should I say, full in myself. Not arrogant. Just good. Really good.

HARNESS THE POWER OF THE HIGH PRIESTESS

Make an altar and be sure you include images and motifs of whatever goddess stirs your soul. Indeed, you may also pay tribute to powerful women in your life. A picture of your grandma, Kate Bush or Oprah are all welcome.

Pray to yourself. Not to god, not to a goddess. Pray to the spirit that you are, the one that inhabits your flesh and your spirit. Ask her to step into your shoes and walk you forward.

DIRTY & DIVINE SPELLWORDS OF THE HIGH PRIESTESS

I create wonder from within. I am she, she is me.

3 — THE EMPRESS

INTUITIVE MEANING

The Empress is the mama bird who will gently preen your feathers as soon as pluck them from your back. She is all and she permits all to be here. Through her all is born and becomes known. It is with her temperament, embedded at our heel, that we are dogged, flogged or empowered. As an archetype she is the earthly feminine, she is all: Queen of Hearts, mountainous peaks of expectation, dark depths of watery soul, the beloved of the universe. She is Mother Earth, Pachamama, and the wise embrace of stardust hovering over us. She is maternity, promoting fraternity and ushering grand, unsolicited, unconditional, uncompromising love.

MY JOURNEY

'She's a black god, she's a black god, she's a black god, God is black.'

Those were the words I awoke to this morning. Not channelled by the ether, but presented to me in song format by my musician husband. He had stayed up into the small hours creating a new song. Those lyrics were the chorus. And it gave me goose bumps. But of course she is.

Prior to this I had awoken wanting to stroll to the local village and buy a rabbit and a tattoo. The rabbit for my eldest daughter, the tattoo, a spiritual affirmation for me. I did neither because the house is a stinking mess and my baby has a cold. I needed instead to make space wherein I can thrive. The Empress is so much more than the purveyor of domestic bliss, but she's got that buttoned down too.

The Empress is an easy one for me. I open myself to her and she flows right in. But I'm a woman, a creative one, and I'm a mother. Not that those things necessitate an Empress. She exists in so many forms. She is the scientist who gently nurtures molecules. The bricklayer who sings his son to sleep so tenderly. The hand that holds yours, the warmth of the sun, the kindness of a smile, the place and people that make you feel safe and welcome. She is the one who roars to defend her project, her craft, her desire. She is the burn within that desires and lusts and craves, because from this place so much can be birthed.

She creates space for growth, for herself, for those she loves. Remember that teacher you adored, who made you feel safe and want to learn? She is her. Your mother, grandmother, your best mate's mum who took you under her wing. The boss who gave a shit and made your life easy. The friend whose home is a second home to you when life gets hard. She is loving power that promotes all growth. All of it.

The Empress is the mother of nature. Her intuition is honed with clay and salt. She births the lot of us like a warrior. Her wisdom comes not from esoteric blatherings, but from the grime, the flora, the living of life. She is our atoms. The Empress is a goddess, an earth-bound one. She is Vesuvius. She is the hurricane, tornado and tsunami. Her love is that cooling breeze that wafts by and takes the heat, just for a second, from your burned flesh. She is a daisy chain. She is Mother Teresa, she is Nala, she is Madonna, Oprah, Gaga, Adele, Hillary, Maya, Ellen, Angelina, Taylor, Kesha, Malala, she is Beyoncé. She only needs one name. Not like a male world that requires a powerful first name followed by some well-endowed surname. She can be known as she is, a few syllables of something less rare than we realise. She is you.

The Empress' feminine streak of power has until recently been denigrated and obscured. Her role has been pushed down under as unimportant, menial, boring and without merit. Yet we would all be lost without her. Her love is so real and so vastly important that she makes and creates whole people and, dependent on her mood, she buoys them up or ruins them. Without her, without a loving mother figure, people struggle through life. She is the bolster to our lives. Without her, without her, without her, we are lost. Her role is all. She is all.

The Empress weaves her magic in silence, in private, in spaces kept shuttered to the world. She wears a burka and schools her children in ways that speak to souls, not necessarily to society. She moves deftly and quietly through misogyny. In recent years her voice has become more pervasive, more intriguing. She has been too easily labelled and stuffed back down, she is careful not to wear a sticker defending herself. She rose lately as 'feminist', but that was torn away from her, made distasteful, attacked and vilified. So now she is creeping in simply as female, as feminine, as a billion different women pursuing a million different injustices.

She is at every corner; she is calling us out. She isn't yelling. She is writing, singing, tweeting and sharing. She is meeting with other females, over cake, in meditation, with coffee and babies, with tea and trumpets. She is coaxing the males into their better power, requesting that they see, do and be better. She is recreating the earth in personal, unique and subtle ways. So small these steps she takes that one day we will turn around and say, 'We women did that... We snuck our lives onto the agenda without it being noticed. We tore down the patriarchy one sentence at a time, one text, one status update, one outfit, one hairy armpit, one truth, one smile, one grimace, one Instagram post at a time.'

She does not go head to head with The Emperor. That failed. She cannot win at his game. Just as he can never win at hers, given the chance. She can only win at her own. She has to figure out how to play, what her rules are. It has been hidden from her for so long. Where she is now, where you are now, is self-love, self-knowledge and a cool, slow negation of anything that fails to be fair. As we swerve towards an inner journey, The Empress guides us to something bigger. She takes us to ourselves, and from here she reminds us of true, connected self, of the influence and power of being a woman.

HARNESS THE POWER OF THE EMPRESS

Search for orgasmic states, be that with a partner or on your own. Seek and you will find. Craft from within that place an all-powerful certainty in yourself, in your feminine being, in your Kali-like ability to love and destroy, birth, build and bury.

Be omnipotent in your every doing. Place yourself upon a pedestal, not with arrogance, but with warmth. Expect truth and be humble.

Wear something extra special, maybe a ring or bracelet you usually retain for 'best'. Every time you notice it on yourself, allow it to remind you that you are always your 'best'.

DIRTY & DIVINE SPELLWORDS OF THE EMPRESS

I am the Goddess.

4 – THE EMPEROR

INTUITIVE MEANING

The Emperor represents male power and the ways it may manifest. Our current experience of him is purveyed through the Patriarchy we live in. Look to your male leaders and there he is, sometimes wise and loving, sometimes cold and warped.

As it stands mankind has come to: continual defence. The lust for more. The need to pursue that which is not in his possession. The use and manipulation of all else to help achieve his own ends. His modern power is underpinned by fear. Who would he be if he was not x, y and z? He is afraid of his soulful truth and his life has become a bulletproof vest to that truth. He could be a whole other kind of patriarchy, though how that looks is a mythical beast for us who are so fully sullied by what the patriarchy of the moment offers.

He has given a lot (civilisation as we currently know it), but he wants back in return, and he may, or may not, allow you your thing (civilisation as it could be imagined from any other perspective). That's the kind of guy he is. Strong, wilful, giving, creative, knowledgable and deeply, deeply entrenched in the survival of his own being..

MY JOURNEY

I've been stuck on this card for a few days. I do struggle with the male cards. I'm so closely aligned to all my female aspects; I find it hard to get truly to grips with all things testicular. The past few days have however seen a struggle for balance in my relationship. We have recently had a baby, and that tends to send things out of whack. I noted yesterday that both my husband and I were complaining of the same thing. Apparently we are both not being very nice to each other.

The thing is, I can see he is trying to be nice to me and vice versa. But life steps in and we get niggly and grouchy and suddenly we are the other's enemy. Our inner Empress and Emperor are attempting to meet in the middle, and failing. Not horrifically, but in a general 'I don't get you' way. The more I think about it, the more I recognize how argumentative we have been these past few days under The Emperor's rule.

I have thought deeply on all the Emperor's traits, that is, what I see as essential to awesome masculinity. I came up with this. Certainty, love, kindness, power used with wisdom, strength, ideas, earthiness combined with a big flash of philosophy. Hang on though, do these traits make an Emperor? Maybe not. Maybe I'm describing an ideal man. But The Emperor, in a good mood is the ideal boss man. He is the president who makes jokes and kisses babies. In a bad mood, he is Hitler. That is the spectrum of his possibilities. Either way he is riding his ego like a firebrand.

I've been saddled by all kinds of practicalities this week. Things I wish an Emperor would come and whisk away. Mortgage renewal being one of them. But Emperors don't help with mortgages: they create them. They sit at the top of the food chain and their underlings sell their products, or their beliefs or their propaganda. They are bankers, they are dictators, they are directors, they are Mr Big, but without quite so much love for Carrie.

I feel like I've buckled a bit under The Emperor. I've come up sick and moaning. I'm pulling on my Empress but there is little Emperor to be seen. Try as I might he isn't showing up for me. I look to my husband, he is pottering, doing his usual thing, not much Emperor going on this week for him either. He has been off work sick too. In between times he thoughtfully allowed me to eat all the strawberries and created amazing music in his studio shed. But he isn't really an Emperor.

We aren't really a household that has Emperor traits. I'm just not feeling him.

I think the reason I struggle with The Emperor is because I struggle with patriarchy. I was brought up by feminists and my

Dad was more an Empress than an Emperor. The Emperor smacks to me of authority and misuse of power, even though, sometimes, that misuse is apparently and allegedly for the greater good.

Equally if we backtrack a day we can reformulate The Empress as less than perfect. I could take my worst traits and align them with her. But I didn't. And yet still even with this self-analysis under my belt I struggle to align an Emperor with anything much good. Maybe it's a sign of the times. Maybe The Emperor and Empress are just very different beasts. Maybe a world run by men is just all too different than one nurtured by women. Maybe my perspective is just too nurturing, because many people would see The Emperor's ego-led, brawn, brain and desire for omnipotence as good things. Our society is built around such power-hungry concepts. It sticks in my throat, literally: my throat is hurting. It's not what I love. I do not love The Emperor, not in his current overwhelming incarnation, the misogyny and the patriarchy that he currently lords over.

Maybe we have yet to see good Emperors. It seems to me that the best men get trodden down beneath the might and grandiosity of a warring Emperor. Men who might represent something more genuine and heartfelt are thrown in jails or executed before they make that kind of mark. The Emperor is just not my type, actually I'll be frank, he can fuck off. I'm done with this card.

You don't have to like all the cards. How you feel has great worth to how you read. You don't need to have textbook understanding, because when a card arises in a reading you are doing, it does so for your interpretation. The universe has a plan. It syncs up with you. Trust your gut.

HARNESS THE POWER OF THE EMPEROR

Call upon the power of The Emperor to guide you in any matters that you feel are beyond you or out of your control. Ask him to step up and power you through. Allow his dictatorial obstinacy to assist as and when it is appropriate. Take him to see your bank manager, divorce lawyer or meeting with your boss.

Think on any traits that you have which may be aligned with the power of The Emperor. Where did you learn them, and who from? Meditate on The Emperors in your life and how they make you feel.

Envision the powerful male. Apply new traits to him. Allow his power to burst forth from your imagination in whatever way your stream of consciousness takes you. Spend some time thinking on men you have known who were powerful, but perhaps didn't fit the patriarchal dialogue.

DIRTY & DIVINE SPELLWORDS OF THE EMPEROR

I am as strong and as powerful as I need to be.

5 – THE HIEROPHANT

INTUITIVE MEANING

The Hierophant represents the wisdom of the past and ambition for the future. Put them together, in this moment, and you get the insight of The Hierophant. He is a man of all ages, an energy of 'better'. He is good, he is great, he is kind. He may be an antidote to the patriarchal side of masculinity that can be jarring. He looks into the past and he improves. The Hierophant may borrow some of his knowing from ancient systems and traditional organisations, but he doesn't enforce them. He is open to difference and likes to grow with the times. He is a philosopher, a priest, a professor, a shaman and a teacher.

When dispossessed of his core spirit, The Hierophant can rely too heavily on rules and institutions. He finds his greatest knowing, his greatest comfort, when he combines the wisdom of many, with the wisdom of his own living.

MY JOURNEY

I wished for a High Priest and this is that guy. I am glad to be out from under a few days of oppression that was The Emperor, and am hoping something more divine might spring. The Emperor held me captive for such a long time, such is his power. The Hierophant is not one to host such inclinations, he pulls his wisdom from the divine. This should be interesting.

Or less than interesting, it seems. Today was a tangle of vomiting kids, having a potent cold myself and strange interactions with a couple of different institutions. The Hierophant does represent organisations and so this is fitting. I had arranged the whole day and mobilised many people so that I could attend an appointment. Only to be called half an hour prior to the meeting with a change of venue. The third in a lack of communications around that very appointment.

So where does The Hierophant come into this messy day? He filters through in the honesty of subsequent communications.

Meanwhile all else has stopped. My eldest daughter has been sick and I'm being parental. And there is no more powerful time to be a parent than when your baby is projectile vomiting all over the living room. It brings forth chunks of memory. Except in that memory I was the child.

The hideous nature of being sick is now my task to soothe. I am holding her hair back, I am filling the hot water bottles, I am helping the baby sleep whilst gently nudging the sickling to drink more water. I am taking very personal stuff from my past and utilising it in the present to bring love and compassion to the children in front of me. I have an eye to the future, too. I can't overreact for fear of placing a fear or phobia of sickness within her. I have to be cool, and tell her she is brave and empathise, commiserate and be compassionate. It's a complex thing, for such a simple event. The Hierophant presides over this with wisdom.

Because that is what The Hierophant does. He takes the best of the past and the highest hopes for the future and he melds them into the present. He ushers them forth, not through the magic of The Magician, but through the tried and tested means of something such as religion, institutions or the catch-all cultural phenomena of parenthood.

HARNESS THE POWER OF THE HIEROPHANT

Draw a life line. Place upon it formative experiences from your past, things that crafted you into who you are currently. Then take that path forward into the future. What do you hope for? How can the life learnings of the past, and hopes in the present, help form that future?

Think on the institutions that have been part of you. Perhaps you were raised in a specific religion. Or maybe a large organisation has played a part in your life as an adult. Consider what positive things you can take from those particular cultures, but recognise that these groups are human and therefore fallible. Recognise where they may have failed you and also open yourself to alternative viewpoints.

DIRTY & DIVINE SPELLWORDS OF THE HIEROPHANT

I am the master of all I have learned.
From here, I can become master of my all.

6 — THE LOVERS

INTUITIVE MEANING

Love tends to be the point of life. As such the complexity of this card is vast. It covers all your interactions, from a stolen kiss through to an 80 year marriage. It is unrequited, it is your stalker, it is tradition, it is the obscure, it is dull and staid, it is kinky and exciting. Essentially, though, love is that thing which we all seek. It sits at the heart of our existence, at the root of all that we are, all that we hope for.

The entwined couple in the image carry within them a thousand possibilities. Are they making love? Are they fighting? Are they seething? Are they faithful? Are they kind? Are they inspiring each other? Are they married or have they just met? If you think you want a lover, then you invite in life, and life is never as easy as Disney Princesses make it appear. You do not set sail into happy-ever-afters. You set sail into something, anything and everything. Those looking for love, or in love, should buckle up and hold on tight.

MY JOURNEY

This is the card that everyone secretly wants, and yet, when they get it, things get complicated. Our expectations of love are wholly out of sync with the reality. The thing about love is that it is an awesome story. What we think it is when we 'fall in love' is a very different thing to that which it turns out to be several years down the line. The myth about love, which tells the young that love is the beginning of life and the end of all things vexing, is debatable. Many weather-worn folks might argue the opposite.

Love is always wonderful in the beginning, or at least it seems better than the state in which we find ourselves prior to meeting another person equally ready to 'fall'. The honeymoon phase of lust, desire, awe and adoration are a heady scent that knocks us for six. We make commitments, years go by and domesticity, routine, the ordinariness of life might catch up with us. That is when love becomes a challenge. We are challenged to love our partners in spite of what we come to see as their flaws. We are challenged to love them in the face of bad behaviour, childhood issues, depression, illness, bad temper, wandering eyes or wilful disregard. Our perfect self also erodes as time and events take their toll. Love becomes a challenge and the longer we stay with a partner, the more we look to the heavens to help guide us along.

It's not all bad though. Love is our most heavenly experience on this planet. We play out many of our most important lifelong lessons with first loves, one time dates, the one that got away, lovers, partners and spouses. Within these formats of togetherness, we learn so much about ourselves, and indeed about each other. We are pushed and pulled, torn apart and pieced together by our lives with these people. Whether relationships last, whether they fail, we are gifted glimpses of some real magic (alongside some hellish lows too). The whole world can be played out within a twosome in ways we never expected when we laid eyes on any particular beloved.

In the end there are too many scenarios, too many love options for me to even try to outline here. You must think upon the loves and lusts you have felt. What did they teach you? Where did they take you: philosophically, internally, emotionally, mentally? Where do you hope a love situation will take you? What do you learn about yourself, your capabilities, your depths, your tolerances, your patterns? Apply all this, then watch, listen to and read any work ever created on love and you still aren't even plumbing the true depths of the scenarios this card can represent. And that is why The Lovers is magic. Because it is everything. It is all our hopes and all our fears and all our middling in-betweens rolled into one.

To interpret this, we must use our gut. We must align this card with the ones that surround it. Just for a moment meditate on what love has taught you, what lesson floats to mind.

I am minded to see the journey of myself and my husband from young wild kiddos, through to the responsibility-laden parents we are now, glazed and exhausted and yet ploughing through, finding new ground and slowly looking forward to when we might again be a little wild for an hour or, if we are lucky, an evening. Love is an ever-changing animal, and we have certainly had highs and plumbed the depths of lows. For us it's been a true journey. . . and continues to be so. Where are you on your journey?

HARNESS THE POWER OF THE LOVERS

Turn the light of love inward. Consider what it is in you that is lovable, not to others, but to yourself. What do you love about you, about being you? Contemplate what you wish for from a lover, then give it to yourself. Take yourself on a date. Take yourself to bed. Take yourself by the hand and show yourself a good time/the world/a glass of prosecco. . .

Contemplate past loves, and instead of placing blame or feeling regret, think instead on what you learned. See purpose in thwarted passion.

DIRTY & DIVINE SPELLWORDS OF THE LOVERS

Love is a heaven of my choosing.

7 – THE CHARIOT

INTUITIVE MEANING

The Chariot is the first non-human card. It is both an energy and a theme. The first theme of the tarot. And it doesn't pretend to be something banal. Rather, The Chariot sums up life: life is so hard, we suck it up, we get on. We triumph time and time again. Every day that we wake up, we overcome our chaos. Some of those chaotic moments will be more searing than others. The key is not to get lost in the pain, but to ride past it, to become more whole as a result of our scars.

The Chariot is raw, bare-knuckled survival. It is becoming through trial and tribulation. It is the evolution of mankind, consistently overcoming disaster, leaving apes in the dust and becoming terrifically empowered. It is riding past heartbreak, fear, anxiety, addiction strolling onward with a soft smile and a swinging hip.

MY JOURNEY

I can see where this is going. This card is perfectly apt for today as already I have had a cry. Already I have felt overwhelmed and swept under by the unfolding events. Already I have harboured grand positivity that this situation is soon to resolve itself for the better. The Chariot is a card of coming through chaos, and coming through it stronger. My particular chaos involves vomiting children and severe dehydration.

Yesterday I took my daughters to the doctor, expecting to be sent home and told that rest was enough. The eldest, who has been suffering from sickness badly for a week was found to be severely dehydrated. I was given an hour to fill her with water and return her for more tests.

Have you ever tried to get a sick-feeling three-year-old to drink? Even under the shadow of hospitalisation, she didn't make it easy. But we got through it. We drank, and I mean we, I was drinking in utter sympathy and partly in the hope that I could perhaps transmute my hydration levels to her. It worked. And after an hour of drinking, followed by her throwing up most of the water, followed by me spilling the vast majority of her urine sample over my bathroom, we returned to the doctor. She was less dehydrated. We then spent another hour in the doctor's surgery. Drinking. Again she was doing better. And since then my life has revolved around getting her to drink.

Whilst this has been going on, my baby has learned to squeal and screech and scream. She does this for everything. She is happy: she squeals, loudly. She is annoyed: she screeches, loudly. She is tired: she screams, loudly. It's been a whole hell of fluids and caterwauling. I'm tired. I really want to watch The Walking Dead, or X Files and zone out to the horror of a fictional world. But I'm seriously on parental duty. So earlier today, I had a little cry.

I never cry. I just don't. It takes a lot to push me to that. I am taking what may only be a few minutes to reflect. The Chariot seems appropriate. If nothing else, it reminds me strongly that I will get through this. I will learn from it too. I will become the keeper of the waters and purveyor of positivity. And I bet a million bucks that later tonight I'll be watching The Walking Dead. I will come out of this stronger and with zombies on the horizon it will all be a memory.

The Chariot is a hero to me today. She shows up to give hope and to put things in perspective. It's a mess, but it won't be for much longer. I can take the reins, be in charge, dispense copious liquids and turn this mess around.

But then, just when I thought things were getting better, they got worse. We were yet again back and forth to the doctors with a dehydrated child. At this point I gave over to the flow. Instead of trying to 'beat the system' and hydrate the little one, I accepted the outcome, no matter what it was going to be. In the end, the universe has greater plans and if she was so sick she needed to be hospitalised, then so be it.

Releasing myself to the circumstances was freeing. I could instead focus on the whole picture, rather than some pithy and obsessive attempts to make a person drink water. I was wholly present and I was able to discuss with her what was happening, what might happen, I packed a hospital bag, got the family mobilised and was ready. As it happened, we were sent home.

From here on in she got better. I rode the lows, embraced the chaos, steeled myself for anything and everything, and came out the other end fighting.

HARNESS THE POWER OF THE CHARIOT:

Make a list of the times in your life that were dark and chaotic. Write a new list of all the skills and self-understanding you gained on the other side of darkness. Keep that somewhere safe to be revisited in times of tumult.

Embrace any current chaos with inner bravado. Know that when it ends, the world will have rearranged itself in intriguing ways.

If you dare to, welcome chaos, invite it, allow it to act on your world as is needed.

DIRTY & DIVINE SPELLWORDS OF THE CHARIOT

I ride my chaos and grow.

8 – STRENGTH

INTUITIVE MEANING

Strength is your ability to endure. To seek within yourself and find, not power, but resilience, and an underlying love that makes all things doable. Strength is the rock upon which so many rely, and indeed it is a place within that keeps you sane amongst the diverse difficulties of life. Strength is a quality, often misunderstood, and yet is inherent amongst us all. It is not the sole fortune of some lucky folk. It is an attribute we are born with. You cannot train your strength. You can only test it. And life will test it. Many times. Often in cruel and unusual ways. You will be tested. It is only here that you can measure your depths.

Strength, in our modern world, has become bed buddies with the likes of aggression, violence, forcefulness and success at all costs. This is not how Strength enters into our life on a daily basis. Indeed, those behaviours feel cold and needy in the light of what they are trying to achieve. You are violent due to lack in yourself, not due to strength. You are aggressive due to needing to push oneself into centre stage, because deep down, you feel ignored, scared and vulnerable.

True strength has no other motive. It exists from a deep inner well of love and spirit. It focuses its power on a belief that all will be well, everything has a purpose, and that love is a healing, motivating, giving force that can cure all. Yet Strength isn't hippy, dippy or trippy. It is ferocious in its desire to be there, to be a rock, to maintain connection, to nurture, to hold, to carry, to support and to heal.

The Strength card speaks to the plummeting well of our inner power. The strength to endure, to hold yourself high, and importantly to give peace and power to others through our own inner resources.

MY JOURNEY

On the day that heralded Strength, I felt anything but strong. I woke up feeling sorry for myself, another day in the sick house, holding it all together. I was staring glumly at my iPad screen, and my eldest daughter was watching what I refer to as 'crap' on my iPhone. My baby girl was chilling happily between us. But we weren't connecting, we weren't being real. We were suffering from lack of strength and substituting it with distraction. I decided simply to change the way I was being. Instead of letting the complaints of my overtired ego get to me, I took control. I wrapped myself and my daughters in a little bubble and said, hey, let's be together, let's do stuff, let's make this day different. In doing this I cured myself and brought us together.

I looked up for new inspiration. I saw that there was a good frost outside. So we all donned our coats and boots and went for a garden adventure. I pulled myself out of my pit and dragged them with me. We continued on this note throughout the day. I took charge, making the day happen, being real, being strong. Pushing outside of my desire to vegetate and creating a new flow.

There are a million ways to harness strength. The key is that it assists us in moving out of any funk we are in, any bad mood, any fear, any self-pity. Strength awakens us to the possibility in every second and crosses us from the dark to the light.

HARNESS THE POWER OF STRENGTH

Welcome the trouble of others as you play and practice at being the calm in their storm.

Dig deep into your own super powers of strength. Offer kindness and warmth to all. Be the smile in a stranger's day that makes all the difference.

Physically challenge yourself. Your physical self is intrinsic to your spiritual being. Go get strong in your body, so that your body can carry the vast power of your divinity!

DIRTY & DIVINE SPELLWORDS OF STRENGTH

I can carry that which calls me.

10 – THE WHEEL OF FORTUNE

INTUITIVE MEANING

The Wheel of Fortune is serendipity and synchronicity. It is the curves that keep things interesting. It is the slips and trips that keep us on our toes. Just when we think we understand the pattern of life, The Wheel of Fortune turns and who knows what calamity or calm may arise. The last time I pulled this card I was on holiday. I arrived in my hotel room and drew back the curtain. Right outside my hotel room window there happened to be a huge Ferris wheel. The Wheel of Fortune, above all else, has a wicked sense of humour. You may choose to ride it laughing or bemoan its spins.

The Wheel is a gamble. We have no say over its course. The only influence we have is over our reaction to The Wheel as it turns. Know that, deep down, the hoops, loops and spins of life are all but a game. The Wheel is urging you to see beyond the nature of fear and to instead root in reality. Yes, that reality contains huge uncertainty, but this is exciting. With the unknown comes so much expectation, hope, desire and, oftentimes, fulfilment. Life on this planet is so full of difficulty, and yet many of us smile through the tears. Many of us take those tears and turn them into foundations. Whatever life is throwing to you right now can be embraced with a whole heart. Step off the insipid hamster wheel of dark thoughts and instead imagine yourself to be atop a beautiful and ornate Ferris wheel, content in your soul and eagerly awaiting the next miraculous turn.

MY JOURNEY

So far today I have done very little. Or at least that is how it seems. The reality is that I have placed myself, not so much on a Wheel of Fortune, but on a wheel of anxiety. I woke with the lovely news that I had very little to do. How lovely, how perfect. Yet almost immediately my mind started to rage and rail against this influx of me-time.

Instead of embracing the nothingness, doing what I used to do so well (bathing, eating, reading, watching Netflix), I started a frustrating internal dialogue about all the other things I could do instead. There are so many options. I could see some friends, who would give me a spark and zest that I so needed. I could go shopping and buy lots of lovely healthy food, after all, the cupboards are pretty bare, and I'm in need of some organic carrots and a fresh start. I could go get that tattoo, because it has spiritual significance and would be a nice gift to myself.

All my thoughts centred around my wellbeing. The things I could do to best promote it. Yet I was ignoring the most obvious thing: I am exhausted. I need to rest. And as boring and unproductive as that seemed, it was what I needed.

The Wheel of Fortune, it seems, is so easily interrupted by our best-laid plans. We too easily take ourselves from the easy flow, and settle instead on some hare-brained idea. It's not the doing, here, that was really the problem. It's the thinking. Or, should I say, the overthinking. I spent a good two exhausted hours, seemingly relaxing, but actually stressing and vexing about relaxing.

In the end I succumbed to the inevitable. I had a quick bath, then got into bed and had a nap. Even then my mind started to rumble with possibilities for later. It was only when I consciously decided to meditate that things slowed down, my mind accepted the choice to do nothing. And then finally, bam, nothing was done. And, oh my, I feel so much better for it.

It is too easy to wrap oneself up in the wheel of anxiety. To allow rampant thoughts to rage across our wellbeing, even when those thoughts purport to be about our wellbeing. The mind is a tricky mistress. It takes cunning and mindfulness to really overcome her wicked ways.

So what does a busy mind have to do with The Wheel of Fortune? I believe it stands in its way. It shoves a big stick between the spokes and stops it spinning. We are so busy trying to take control of our lives we don't allow things to organically arise. We stop the flow and create a dam. When that dam breaks, all hell is let loose. Yet we were the ones who stopped things with our ever-churning perspective, plans and decisions.

When I was laying in the bed with my baby girl today she stared into my eyes and I stared right back. There was no awkwardness, no weird need to look away, nothing was being interpreted. We simply looked into each other's being. There was no underlying subtext, no need, no misunderstandings. This was so peaceful and it made me realise that we come into this world free from anxiety. We have no expectations. We have some demand that our basic needs are met, but beyond that, we are so open.

As life goes on we accumulate thoughts and choices and we act upon these daily. Soon these thoughts shift and can easily tip over into vexation and anxiety. We are no longer thinking, we are painfully ruminating, as if the act of thought alone can change our life. We overrule our basic needs with what we have thought up. But we are simply wallpapering over our own cracks. They come back to get us in the end. The Wheel eventually powers past the stick, snapping it, releasing the backlog of life upon us in one fell swoop.

I have often seen The Wheel of Fortune as the card that represents surprise and the unexpected. But today I saw it differently. It offered me a glimpse of what happens when you become too controlled and allow your mind to be the driver. What happens is that all the lovely surprise and unexpected flow of all kinds of wonderful just don't show up. And it is all our own doing.

Cease the thinking and tune into the underlying message. Abide by that and allow life to take you where you haven't thought of yet. Herein lies one of the secrets of intuition: it is not the voice in your head, it is the sleepy, quiet slumbering sound of your soul. She is too easily switched off in favour of the 'I should' and 'I will'. If you listen carefully she is the one strongly, peacefully saying something more definite. Start from that point and allow the rest to stream onward.

HARNESS THE POWER OF THE WHEEL OF FORTUNE

Remember back ten or twenty years. Think carefully on those things that brought joy and those that brought sadness. Consider those things now. Were they blockages, or were they building blocks to a brighter future? How have they played a part in making you stronger, better and more you? Contemplate this deeply and, in various areas of your life, choose only to see the powerful and poignant hoops of your life.

Carefully examine your thoughts as they arise. Do they marry up with how you feel? Are you letting them rule, or are you following something more subtle?

What about synchronicity, serendipity and outright crazy coincidence? How has The Wheel brought all kinds of unexpected fairy-dust tinted events to your life? Expect more. Ask for more. Allow them to arise by getting out into the world and saying yes to opportunity.

DIRTY & DIVINE SPELLWORDS OF
THE WHEEL OF FORTUNE

I embrace each turn of my life with love, laughter,
humour and hope.

9 — THE HERMIT

INTUITIVE MEANING

The Hermit is not so much about being lonely, as taking time to be solo, to be one, to seek inside. The Hermit does not seek foreign shores for self, for spirit or for wisdom, he finds it within. He shuns the common knowledge to discover what he himself already knows.

We are told by society that we are born knowing nothing and therefore we must accumulate it from external sources. The Hermit has found that, indeed, the source of knowledge, true knowledge, is within. He may seem a little odd to a world that expects 'all' to be in the pages of a book or in the hands of 'experts'. Yet what he learns from within can be a guiding light to those same people. He can write the books, and inspire others to do the same. He goes within, to give out. He asks you to do the same.

MY JOURNEY

The Hermit asks us to look inside to find our light. One way of doing that is by living in the moment. Although, as a mother to very young children, I am often living in their moment, rather than mine. Scratching out some time to be in my moment is difficult.

I am finding that undertaking this 78-day journey is the introspection I sorely need. I started off this path thinking it might bring external magic and miracles into my life. I hoped for crazy synchronicity, signs and blessings. That would be too easy though, right? The lessons I am learning are the ones that exist beneath the tumult of running and supporting a family. The things I truly seek — peace, love, stability — are not to be found via some external force, some Prince Charming of circumstance, but rather, they bubble up from within.

This time spent alone, in the company of tiny folk, is stirring up so much for me. I am pushed to my limits as I craft their day, provide for their needs, and, at some point, find a way to make myself matter in that equation. In making myself matter, in doing what I love, in reaching into my archives of self, I am becoming better, more self-aware, increasingly in a state of love, not simply towards the people in my care, but towards the soul of me, also in my care.

Before I had any responsibility I made a habit of going to bed early, just so I could lay and think, for hour upon hour. I didn't have much to be up for (college maybe) and I would take much pleasure in my time to daydream. Looking back on it I can't imagine what I spent hour upon hour thinking about. I am guessing that it was in part meditative. In another part it was downloading my day. Perhaps, in a very teenage way, I was planning and fantasising my inevitable romance with Robbie Williams. Whatever it was, it was mine. An adult life has taken over that very personal inner passage of self. I don't often get to play any of those thoughts out. My thinking these days has function. And function becomes stress all too easily. I'm always trying to solve something.

So in the evening of The Hermit I put the kids to bed and went downstairs to see my husband. He was fast asleep. I tried to wake him. He didn't stir. So I got all teenage. I went and had a hot bath with a good book. Then I went and lay naked on my bedroom floor. Why the floor? Because it felt real. Laying naked on the floor (instead of the bed) felt, in that moment radical, it felt like I was me again. Teenagers don't need furniture. They don't get comfy, they strike a pose, they resist the smug, snug of duvets and memory foam and they find bricks to perch gloriously upon.

Laying on that floor I didn't waft off into fantasy. I'm a little too far past that. I brought my thoughts round to power. Instead of trying to solve my problems, I circumnavigated them. I lay there thinking: *I am rich, abundant and healthy.* All at once challenging my habits of poverty, lack and a creeping sugar habit. I am rich, abundant and healthy. Once upon a time I'd balk at that list. It's not societally worthy or spiritually wholesome is it? Or is it. . . ? But then I'm up against a maternity leave situation and a soon to be lack of money and a huge desire to be with my little ones for an extended period. So, instead of resolving to solve it, I'm expecting to instead.

Find yourself a patch of floor and announce what you are. Because you are what you think. Dig deep for your reasoning. Then grow it, starting with naked belief, faith and trust.

HARNESS THE POWER OF THE HERMIT

Be alone, even in company. Recognise that the most important connection you can foster is the one to yourself. How do you feel at any given moment? Embrace it, don't dismiss it: it holds a vast education. If you feel awkward, shy, afraid or joyful, explore that. Create an internal dialogue that is meaningful and that allows your ability to thrive in your own physical environment. Own your truth, acknowledge it within, be in her.

Take some purposeful time out. Five minutes in the garden, a silent meditative walk to the shops, take a yoga class, paint, cook, draw, colour, breathe. In this space go within.

DIRTY & DIVINE SPELLWORDS OF THE HERMIT

I go within to experience all that I am.

11 – JUSTICE

INTUITIVE MEANING

We are often knocked off our paths by the circumstances we are born into and then again by the events that happen to us and the situations we create. Justice acts to amend all of this and resituate us where we should be. It can feel bitter. It can feel beautiful. It plays out through a million different outlets and is inevitable. We are all recipients and creators of Justice. We bow to it, we are its beneficiaries, we are its actors, playing it out powerfully with every thought, action and breath.

If ill-placed, we rail against it. Perhaps sometimes we don't recognise it, and see it instead as unfairness. Other times we shiver in its shadow, as if we expected life to be so different. Whether we shiver, shake or shimmy to the thrall of Justice, know that one way or another, it will come. To you, to us, to the cogs of the grimy civilisation we inhabit. It is like a stealthy and invisible ecosystem, it amends itself, always, through flies, maggots, angel wings and synchronicity, it finds its way.

MY JOURNEY

The energy of Justice has been with me for a few days and it is far subtler than I expected. Our modern society associates Justice with the penal system, with punishment and penalty. But the feeling of this card is more karmic, perhaps even more subtle than karma. Justice is the universe righting itself and there is nothing you or I or Judge Judy can do about it. Justice has nothing to do with comeuppance and everything to do with balance, empowerment and self-love.

Yet I am finding this card really difficult to capture. It pervades everything and in its wisdom, it becomes flighty, invisible almost.

Justice, it seems, is not the pomp and circumstance the modern world rallies. Nor is it vengeful or spiteful correction. I'm not sure it is even redemptive. It simply is. It is a gentle lullaby pulling us so softly back to what 'should be'.

The consistent thing, since this card designed my days, is that I feel strongly reminded of precisely what I want, and why I want it. All the excess has dropped away and I'm feeling clear. I can feel the truth that resides under all the other truths. My focus has sharpened and I am more acutely conscious of purpose. And it is much simpler than I thought. I am simpler. What I need is rather easy. The way to achieve it is not by over-complication, overthinking or shrouding myself in possibility. I must simply move towards my goals, with faith, love, trust and without excess.

I have felt something brewing lately. My thoughts have taken a turn away from reading the cards, and instead I am focused on reading life, understanding it. This book has altered. It has moved from being an understanding of how to read the cards, into something far more powerful. Justice has realigned me with something bigger. The archaic primal energies of self are flooding through and I am encouraged in this by advice from those who have read the book.

It must be bigger. It must be more. It must find new depths and heights. The balance is there to be struck, whipped into a frenzy and assimilated upon these pages. What you have read thus far is not what you would have read had I finished writing the book yesterday. Editing has slashed the word count in half and added guts instead. Justice has played herself out and spoken through me. Everything has changed. And yet it has not. How subtle.

I am minded also to consider the theme of justice more broadly. We live, it seems, in unjust times. And yet, didn't our parents always warn us that life is not fair? Mine did. Justice is so powerfully focused these days through the channel of social media. As I type, so many opposing opinions butt heads and play themselves out on timelines and newsfeeds worldwide. The one compelling thing about this is the variation in what is perceived as justice, and just how strong the feelings are regarding that. I feel that perhaps the enacting of justice through human means, is sand to the wind: passing and meaningless.

Natural justice, karma, the inevitability of chaos. Now that is interesting justice. And it is through chaos that much is restored to some semblance of order. We must experience the fire and tornados first, though. And herein we find even that version of justice unfair. Why should our lives be tumultuous? And yet they are, time and time again, year after year, generation by generation. We live in denial of it. We act surprised when life pulls us in some unexpected direction. We entertain the illusion that we are in control, right up until the tornado is upon us. And then we bemoan it. Only in retrospect may we see how there was sense to it.

True justice is unplanned, unseen, and unexpected. Human justice, the events we make happen, criminal justice, justice by newspaper, justice via gossip, justice through public opinion, violent reparation, they are just human propaganda on a variety of different levels. Such propaganda makes us feel safe, freed from retribution as we watch and comment on the karmic inevitability of others.

Did that celebrity get what she deserved? Was that war justified? Did the vote swing the right or wrong way? Whose lives matter? Did he really bring it on himself? It's all played out through memes and headlines and blogs and two minute interviews. It's all sand between our toes. What comes after our opinion, after our interactions, what comes of all of that? Therein lies the true justice. Our thoughts are part of the storm. Justice blows the winds in and then away and leaves us with something altogether different.

HARNESS THE POWER OF JUSTICE

Get the balance right. Turn yourself on and off as your body and emotions require. Do not power through. Respect your innate needs. Trust that being 'on' all the time is not necessary. Being 'off' feeds and motivates your soul equally.

What guts do you need to spill? Where can you exhibit yourself better? Justice cannot align you unless you stand raw in her light. Open yourself to reframing.

Consider the theme of justice in the world today. What is going on? What is choking up word space on your newsfeed, your newspaper, your radio? How is it 'just' to you? How does it reflect your inner experience?

Play with this idea. . . Imagine that everything you believe to be just, is wrong. Pick another belief, somebody else's, pretend for a few moments that they are right. Shuffle into their beliefs, conjure their reasons.

DIRTY & DIVINE SPELLWORDS OF JUSTICE

I allow justice, in its most raw, natural form to carry me.

12 – THE HANGED MAN

INTUITIVE MEANING

The Hanged Man is fervent in his passions yet stuck in his situation, for now. He can't quite figure or ferment the next move. Yet, whilst in this place of stasis, he will dream, meditate and plan. He is able to look around and be inspired by what he sees, who he sees and those things that occur around him. He must trust that his time to move will come, but for now he hangs aloft, allowing only the passion within to stir.

MY JOURNEY

I am in a place of stasis, of course I am. Yet the ideas flooding into me are voracious in their desire to be heard. I am shocked by the depths of myself that are asking to be plundered for this very journey. Just today, whilst stuck in traffic, the inner path was very much alive and moving forward. My world was alight with self, things I've done, aspects of my incarnation that I will share, in time, on these pages.

My view from this place of limbo is ecstatic and fascinating. On the outside I am clearly tied to my important childcare commitments and daily routine. On the inside I am dreaming up prose, burning with ambition and excitedly combing through the annals of my life as this very inward cauldron of self simmers.

This brings to mind for me the very real struggle of women throughout the age of misogyny. For centuries we have been captured, hanged women, destined to breed and be possessed, unable, unwilling to move, unknown in our own skin. Even our pivotal role as 'mother' has been denigrated to such an extent that we married into servitude, to take no public joy in the love of our children. To be an automaton of life, rather than a skilled and loving purveyor of it.

How must those women's inner lives have looked and felt? Did they burn with fantasy? Or were the dreams careworn right out of them? Did their function as servants and slaves to husbands, workhouses and fields leave them feeling disempowered within their own flesh? Did they shut down, left to rot from the inside out? And for those who didn't marry, who didn't or couldn't have children, those who were not suitably empowered, were these the witches, the whores, the women of ill repute? Was there joy in this for them? Or did their acts of passion set them alight, literally, were they killed — burned or hanged — for what they said and did? Perhaps we are them reincarnate. This lifetime we are more ready to seek deeply, and to move powerfully, biding our time as we stretch the realms of our imagination within, and then beyond, the stasis.

We do our sisters of the past credit by choosing to wallow in our internal world. Unlike them, we can push forward with passions and plans, when the time is right. It is essential we embrace the luxury of time to cultivate self, in the deep appreciation that we have the option.

HARNESS THE POWER OF THE HANGED MAN

Wherever you are in life that is stationary and stuck, let it be. Don't try to plough through brick walls. Stay contentedly in the moment and instead of forcing external movement, look within instead. How do you feel? What can you see? Where are you inspired? Allow your soul to speak to you without the requirement for this conversation to lead anywhere.

If you are normally chock full of action and ideas, step back for a moment. Actively watch and listen to those around you. Smile and nod, but keep your reactions to yourself. Let your opinions remain unsaid, just for once, just to see what happens.

Embrace some boredom. Crack open a big fat jar of nothing. Put your phone/computer aside. Turn Netflix off. Resist the urge to open a magazine or book. Be bored. See what flickers to life within when all distractions are waylaid.

DIRTY & DIVINE SPELLWORDS OF THE HANGED MAN

Where I am, is where it is at.

13 — DEATH

INTUITIVE MEANING

Outside of the obviousness of literal death, this is a card of closure and opening. When one life ends, those that are left begin again. When one situation ceases, a new one replaces it. When there is darkness, soon there will be light.

Death is unavoidable, we meet it every day, and it brings great gifts. Whilst endings can be sorrowful, and death can fill us with dread, the certainty is that life follows. If we apply this to all deaths, then we might know that as spirit, we don't die, we transform. Somewhere out there our beloveds are exalting in a fresh state, just as we, in their absence, revisit life in a new way.

MY JOURNEY

I have spent the past 25 years reassuring those I read for (and myself) that Death does not mean death. Not literally. Yet, of course, if the cards do reflect real life, then sometimes Death means death. Of course it does. It's not a curse, it's not a harbinger of doom, it's just the way that things are. So I go into this day with trepidation and slightly bated breath.

Nana did not die today. It is important to note that fact. What did happen was that it seemed likely, for a few dreadful hours, that she would. My mother-in-law was staying at our house in preparation for an early start together the next day. At 12.30am I was awake with the children. At 1.30am, just as the baby was settling back down again, my husband came in and in a deadpan manner said, 'If you hear noise downstairs it's an ambulance for my mum, she thinks she is having a heart attack.'

I sat for the next hour awaiting that ambulance, stroking her back, reminding her to breathe deeply and attempting to stave off a potential cardiac arrest with energy healing. I'll cut this short. It turns out she was fine. But an event such as that does not just slip out of the mind though, it stays with you, it toys with your perception of the world and it brings one's own mortality into the room.

This 'near death' experience, happening as it did on the day of Death in my journey was poignant. I have been left thinking about life as a result. It's funny how lingering too long on the subject of this mortal coil can send your thoughts spiralling. My thoughts twisted away from death, but more towards what I want out of life. Who I am, who I can become, what I need to put into place to be living the kind of life I hope for. This extended outside of ambition or hope for myself. Instead I was thinking of my grandchildren. I want to be healthy for them. I don't want to be sat on my children's sofa aged 64, with the grandkids in bed, potentially suffering a heart attack.

You might question how I could avoid the inevitable onslaught of aging and health matters. Well, I believe that our health starts in our minds. We don't become old, we age. But many people become old because they don't see that they have any other option. Similarly, we don't become infirm, we become elderly. Again, folks see those two as one and the same result. But they are not. Elderly reflects a time period of life, infirm mirrors the state of health. I'm cool with aging and becoming elderly. I'm not down with being old and infirm.

When I reach the third arm of the maiden, mother and crone triad, I want to live long enough and well enough to spread some of my aged wisdom. If I die in advance of that, then I want to say I made the most of life as it came to me. It's simple: I want to live well. I want to exist healthily. I want to push my body as far as it can and will go and I want to do so with a healthy love of life.

Death is not to be feared. What happens on the other side of it is not important. What truly matters is that we embrace the day, second by second. We must give ourselves the chance, daily, to get the most from where we are.

I look forward to aging, really I do. I am going to be the most fun, the wackiest, the wisest old gal around. It's my intention. I'm making it. I want to be a crone, full of wrinkles and whimsy. It is my true hope that I can reach that stage and when I do I will take it on with wicked humour.

Death has brought me this perspective. It feels light, when I feared it might be heavy. It feels fun, when I thought it might be horror-filled. Death, it seems, is an inspirational figure, waiting for us to see him so that we might see ourselves more fully.

HARNESS THE POWER OF DEATH

Count the little deaths that frequent your day. Each death is followed by an intake of new breath. As space is cleared, it is filled. Examine how this arises in all that goes and comes to you.

DIRTY & DIVINE SPELLWORDS OF DEATH

Death brings my life.

16 — THE TOWER

INTUITIVE MEANING

The Tower is a tower of power. The image upon it looks dire. Everyone flings themselves from its heights as it burns and lightning strikes. Yet the Tower itself is unchanged. It takes it all and remains strong, remains standing.

Life may crumble around you. Folks may fling themselves, lost in drama, from the balustrade. Yet there is a solidity within you. An ability to endure all things. The Tower reminds us that when life becomes hostile, vengeful and crazy, we have a home within, we have a choice, we have limitless strength.

MY JOURNEY

Today isn't even The Tower. I've skipped ahead two days. Today was supposed to be Temperance, and then, after that, The Devil. But somehow it felt more of a Tower day. I went with that and will revisit those others next. (Feel free to institute your own order to your journey should the need take you). I am feeling swirled around in the minor chaos that surrounds me. In the aftermath of my mother-in-law's heart scare last week, my husband is flailing. He has parent issues, like many of us do, and this particular episode has set them off.

My husband suffers occasional depression.

There has been a vast improvement over the years. He has put the work in to get better. Yet sometimes, when he flounders, I find myself resenting the situation. I wonder what it's like to have a partner without depression. I wish he could heal and become whole. I almost slip into being a victim. Almost. Or maybe I do...

But then I see the journey we have taken together, and it has been intense. He is more than just a guy who occasionally fails to cope. He is a creative, he is generous, he is damned handy and he is funny. As a dad he is awesome. He brings me chocolate without me asking and takes the kids so I can have space and time. So I solidify my Tower again so that all those who flail around me in uncertainty can find a home.

Life is fucking hard, I grant you that. I have always coped scarily well with it. I had some teenage angst, some early adult vexations. All my own doing. Once I recognised that fact I fell into place with myself. I've been lucky to be pretty emotionally stable, always. I feel deeply, when it is appropriate, but the rest of the time I'm happy-go-lucky. I allow people their flaws and continue onwards in trust. I can go deeper on my spiritual journey because I recognise the learning in all things.

I've lead a charmed existence, and even the crappy stuff has somehow added to the magical mix. I'm hugely positive. Possibly irritatingly so. I just don't see pain, I see passage. I don't see mistakes, I see space for miracles. I don't see trauma, I see The Tower, a place within, that we all have, where everything can be okay, if we allow it.

So I'm sat here typing this whilst my husband feeds and plays with our eldest. He is a good dude. I'm a good dude. Life will occasionally have us flailing for an answer, a meaning, a purpose, a moment to sulk. But for those who flail, there is always a home. It lays within. In our heart. In our soul. In the generosity of our spirit to see our loved ones and love simply in spite of whatever burdens them. The Tower is wild and worthy. We all are.

One thing in life that we can be assured of is the pain of other people. There is untold suffering and at times we need to be the sacred light in their storm. At times we too will require such a beacon to help deliver us to safety and sanity. A hand to hold, a guiding word, a kindness, a place to shelter and time given from one person to another to help our revival. The Tower is not a card cursed by suffering, it is the stepping stone away from that place of dismal need.

Today, with the backdrop of flooding in the village and a slow spattering of rain against a murky grey sky, I saw my husband gently slipping into his own malaise. Instead of scolding or threatening him, I simply offered love. A part of me felt wounded, but I licked the wound and carried on. It's not about me. It's his pain, his burden and what he brings to our lives far outweighs this. Nor is it helpful for me to become weighed down in the drama of it. Experience has taught me that taking it personally simply makes it worse, adds to the chaos and inflicts new scars on top of old.

Choosing to be a tower of strength diffuses and displaces the upset. It places the drama in its rightful place, with my husband, and challenges him to deal with his own situation. A loving reaction, as opposed to an upset one, adds wisdom to the difficulty we face together. I don't need to carry him. I don't need to give him a solution. I simply need to be, open, non-judgemental, a harbour. From here he is empowered to do whatever he needs to do. So, for now, the drama subsides.

The floods are abating. I'm standing tall, in my kitchen, being the heart of the home, writing a book, looking towards the pile of washing up and knowing that the limitations of domesticity, the mundanity of it all, can indeed be the shining constellations of our lives. Even in the grit, in the daily grind of heartache and backache, and gas men knocking the door whilst I'm mid-sentence and boob out, baby on, I am the Tower. The Tower is me.

HARNESS THE POWER OF THE TOWER

Choose not to react. Breathe, listen, respond with love. Be safe harbour to those in distress.

Count the times somebody was your light in the dark. Give silent and sacred thanks to those who have harboured and sheltered you. There may be many times and people too easily forgotten in the melee of life. Hold them close in your thoughts now. Give thanks to the goddess within and without for connecting their heart to yours.

DIRTY & DIVINE SPELLWORDS OF THE TOWER

My purpose is peace.

17 – THE STAR

INTUITIVE MEANING

A star is but a small prick of light in a night sky. Yet that spark of small nothing is in fact a fiery combustion of universal matter. Its mystical, physical, luminary presence has lorded over hundreds of generations, guiding us, sometimes literally, other times figuratively, through life. The Star doesn't need to come down to

Earth and flaunt its flame, it simply is. And we gaze up in wonder anyway. We trust it is astonishing, no proof is required.

There is you. And then there is the real you, the one who is buried under labels and layers, attitudes and perception. Transformation from a place of whole, honest being is possible when we explore our raw, honest, vulnerable truth. Drop your many disguises. There is better, badder and bolder within. It takes bravery to be the truthful you. The Star asks you to be naked and to reveal your all. Only from here can you follow the light that was ever yours.

The Star is a celestial entity, effectively (and as far as we understand) stars are genderless. Yet her image in Tarot is always female. She is posted in the nude and she is lifting water from one place to another. She is transforming and turning the world around her. She does so in her nude state as a statement of truth. As women born of a modern patriarchy we have been stripped down to nothing but the physical, the nude. Yet this nude, The Star's nude, is one that is not for the consumption of the eye. It is the naked soul. The revealed, bare, truly open self. For us women of the dirty and divine, her message is simple: In your honest to goodness self, in your flesh, in your embarrassment, in your humility, that, my shining stars, is where you find your power.

MY JOURNEY

'Life's not worth a damn, till you can shout out, I am what I am.' These words have been singing round my head since the day of The Star began. I didn't recognise their significance, until just now. So I rushed to my computer to see what card I was on. And perfectly, succinctly, wonderfully, it is The Star.

But what I had hoped would be a day full of starlight, sparkle and shimmering loveliness has warped into something raw and dark. Raw like a fucking sliced open pig, steaming and unbandaged, festering in the heat.

Yesterday I was the Tower, strong for another. Strong so that I did not make the immediate situation worse. That worked, it allowed for the day to go by unsullied. But as the day passed my husband's mood darkened, and he finished it sleeping on the sofa. We didn't argue. We barely spoke. His depression descended like a ghostly funk whilst I played happy families upstairs. Playing, laughing with my children, washing them, feeding them, putting them to bed, ignoring the gloom emanating from the living room.

I don't want to talk about depression. I could. But that's not my thing, it's his. My thing is being privy to this, time and time again. Privy to the weeks of heartfelt loving wonderfulness. Privy to the occasional decline to something morose and haunting. Privy to his anger at the past. Privy to my displays of solidarity, my aching longing for a simpler, steady life. Privy to my hope for a life less ordinary.

I have a habit of living in the moment, something which of course is wonderfully worthy. But it doesn't feel worthy when living in the moment makes you forget the shit that went before, and then it rears its head again and before I know it we are back at square one. And this has been going on for years. Since the beginning when our relationship was conceived in an ecstatic vodka fog. Fourteen years of my varying tolerance and attempted treatment of his depression. Fourteen years trying to get out from under something that in the first place was part of the fun.

My naked self has become covered in all that he brought to me. As is the case for so many women (and men). And whilst much of it has been wonderful, there is still the remnants of those early constellations playing in and around us, guiding us wrongly backwards and sideways and never quite as forward as I would like. I have yet to step fully into my naked raw truth. Perhaps this journey is the stripping salve I need.

I'm not sure if this will make the book. Though it probably should. As this is my most personal feeling, my potent inner poison. I am spiritual, I am happy, I have all I need and want, and yet, I am in this situation that is so difficult. I love my husband, he is a good man, a kind man, a great dad. Yet the cycle we are in, the slow burn into misery, the lack of communication when depression takes hold. It's fucking hard. But hang on a second, this is about me. This journey is about me.

So here is my most honest truth. I say I'm coping, that I'm strong, but the other woman inside does not want to be in this situation any more. One way or another the cycle is exhausting. I'm not very good at coping with this. Not very good at all. I declare that I am a tower of strength, but apparently that tower is built on sand because as soon as it is challenged, I crumble. It's not an obvious thing. My crumbling is very much internal. I smile, I look the same, I run through my day as per normal. Inside I am a steaming turd full of resentment and venom.

I can run a whole gamut of emotions in the face of his depression. I act strong, I am strong. Until suddenly I'm not and I'm bubbling with a million solutions. He might not fix overnight, so then I start to take it personally. Which is when I begin to think of separation and divorce, as if cutting out the wound would extricate me from having to deal with all this... Then I come round, and I'm all divine and loving, intermittent with misunderstanding and lack of understanding, and then back to smiling for the kids.

Just so many feelings.

Everything I said on the day of The Tower, about being emotionally stable, being happy-go-lucky. That is clearly not the case, not every day, not under this particular influence. I really believed I was all sweetness and light. But having to face this all here, I see something different. I'm just as cursed with temper and frustration as anyone else: I suffer, I vexate, I struggle, I bleed.

My feelings are valid. But they aren't necessarily real. I conjure them subconsciously. I grow them from nothing. My good intentions twist, and there I am, suddenly, suffering, letting the dark in, becoming horribly toxic.

The Star is about unveiling our deepest truths. Which is evidently a complex and multifaceted thing if my last comments are anything to go by. Perhaps I would be better airing this to my husband. Though if I do then I am adding to his problems, adding to his woe. So I type them here instead, to share with you, to take to the universe, in the goddess-given hope that I might find a way forward. As right at this moment, I just don't know. I don't want to be in this internal limbo any more. I don't want to be my own toxicity. I need to be able to see a bigger picture, I need to find my divine and cease my inner wailing over the dirty.

If The Star is a deity, an archetype of the raw divine feminine energy, then I pray to her now. I pray for solution, resolution, movement, improvement, healing and love. For us all in this house. But more for me. Fuck it. I pray for me.

HARNESS THE POWER OF THE STAR

Get deep and ask yourself what you really want, need and desire. What is making you happy? What is making you sad? Face it head on. Don't gloss over it, don't edit it.

Spill your guts. If something is upsetting you, or causing you discomfort, find a way to express yourself. Even if that makes the situation feel even more uncomfortable, trust that, in the long term, speaking from your heart is the best way to go.

Find a star in the sky. Wish upon it.

DIRTY & DIVINE SPELLWORDS OF THE STAR

I am what I am.

18 — THE MOON

INTUITIVE MEANING

The Moon illuminates our shadow, our heart, our deepest, weirdest and most uncomfortable self. She doesn't do this for kicks. She does it to enlighten us about our true self, so that we may grow. This is a deeply feminine card. The light she casts, shows you blocks to your divinity. She asks you to embrace the dark night of the soul and to shift accordingly. She guides us through life, raising our pain so that we may manifest our highest self to vanquish it.

The Moon, like The Star, sits high above us in the heavens. Yet their influence, apparently so far removed, is real. The Moon acts to pull at our strings, our tides, our hormones. She is cited as causing werewolves and temporary insanity. Werewolves may be questionable, but drawing out our crazy seems reasonable. And, in doing so, in showing us our dark, in reflecting our deepest being, she acts as a mirror to all that we are. The Star asks us to strip bare. The Moon asks us to delve inside that nakedness and draw our splinters to the surface.

MY JOURNEY

Last night I dreamed that my husband and I were on a roller coaster. It was supposed to be the most exhilarating new ride. But it wasn't, it was dull, boring and nothing really happened. When we got off we realised that we had the power to influence the ride all along. By leaning, pushing and pulling with our bodies we could make the ride better, we could make it awesome. At first my husband railed at the ride staff, why hadn't they told us? But then maybe we were supposed to figure that out ourselves. . .

I woke to my husband taking me in his arms and hugging me

tightly. We chatted honestly. I told him how I felt. He told me how he felt.

Last night was a Pisces new moon. The moon has such a strong influence on the people it shines upon. When I worked in public service complaints we always found that the repeat complainants, the ones who had the kookiest, strangest, most unreal issues, would come out around the time of a full moon. It was then that we would receive lengthy, crazed letters, or desperate, nonsensical phone calls that were impossible to end. A full moon casts its light on all our sides, it is when our inner she-wolf comes out to howl.

But a new moon is different. She heralds growth and new beginnings. Oh, how I'd love to grow and find a new beginning right now. Last night sucked. The things I felt, raw with frustration, embittered by the vicious cycle, were dire.

I went to speak to my husband, I was serious, aching inside. I told him, 'we are caught in a trap'. The Elvis tune by that name struck up in my head and as seriously as I tried to take it we both burst out laughing.

'Because I love you too much baby.'

Sometimes in the midst of something deep and meaningful, the light cracks through. I do truly believe that once we leave this Earth, the stresses and strains of it are but a joke to the soul. We doubtless find the time given to anxiety and worry to be something unreal, something humorous. Perhaps that is why the moon illuminates our tragedies, she is not of this Earth: she is objective, she can show us that a molehill is not a mountain. If we bask in her eerie glow, she can whisper us a thousand truths.

I love my husband. Relationships are hard. Every time I felt stressed over the past few days I inhaled chocolate. Despite a solemn vow to myself to quit sugar. I did it because I could, and I did it in secret, and it made me feel better and worse. Each of us is only ever responsible for our own doings. I can't change him. He keeps buying me chocolate, so clearly he doesn't want to change me.

The life we live internally is often the hardest, the weirdest. He suffers with depression, and I allow myself to get blown into suffering alongside him. It's quite silly, comical really. Who I am on the outside and on the inside can be very different people. I get lost in the moment. Perhaps I ought to ride my roller coaster differently. It is a new dawn, a new day, and I'm not sure if I'm feeling good. Perhaps I am.

If I have learned anything from my spiritual wanderings, it is that we can't alter another person. The most we can do is lead by example. Of late mine and my husband's problems are borne out of mundanity and boring familial domesticity. A few years ago they were derived from wild nights and rock 'n' roll. The lows are far less dramatic these days. They are niggling, bickering and lingering resentments. They are so passé, so freaking conventional. At least when we argued with a hangover or comedown there were fireworks, I don't miss those fireworks of drunken misunderstanding. These days it is the dire task of raking over conversations, 'but you said this', and 'you said that' and 'it wasn't what you said it was the way you said it'.

I don't want to play our relationship out any more on this page. This happens. It is getting better. We work our way through and make efforts to do better, to grow. It's so hard to write about this and to make it public. But with depression being a force that hits one in three people, how can I gloss over it? It's a fierce reality. It's a reality even in the household of the divine mama, the sacred feminine, the spiritualista. It's a reality. It's my reality, to be here. Until the day we float off into the ether, life will hound us.

I share this for another reason. There is a typography of spiritual thought that suggests that when things get hard or 'toxic' you should bail. Here you find refuge in India, or the local ashram, or yoga, or speed dating. It's never that simple. Our love life reflects our light and our dark and there is a great deal of self-deception in thinking otherwise. Love is a heartache, and a bolster. It can be at once a life raft and the stone weighing us down, keeping us stuck in a suspended state of something.

Many of you will be experiencing something similar. The inevitable rut of monogamy, the realisation that people aren't perfect, yourself included. The problems that aren't major, that are easily concealed, but that change everything. The issues that go away for weeks or months, then crop up and ravage the landscape. We keep still and silent, clinging to the good, light and happier times. Yet our dirty secrets, our real issues lurk just beneath, only examined in dark nights of the soul, forgotten when the sun comes up, the chickens rise and something sweeter takes over.

It is for us to push and pull to create something different. It is not our place to change another but we can take aim at ourselves. We can hold ourselves to higher standards, commit to them and see what happens next... With a new moon above, and Elvis charging through my head like a spirit guide, I stand between a place of loss and laughter, lodged firmly between dirty and divine. I'm going to choose dirty old, divine young Elvis, I'm going to aim for comedy, lightness, love. Love is my only target. So I bluster onward, spiritual, human, lit by a new moon, placing faith forward to light my steps with rhinestones and hair grease.

HARNESS THE POWER OF THE MOON

Keep a watchful eye on the phases of the moon. Note significant times in a diary. Notice how you feel around a full and new moon. Sync in with her wisdom.

Meditate beneath her. Spend time in her rays and gaze upon her glory. Ask her to grace you with objectivity.

DIRTY & DIVINE SPELLWORDS OF THE MOON

There is no trap: the escape lies within.

14 — TEMPERANCE

INTUITIVE MEANING

Temperance is very much about balance. He asks that we curb our temptations. That we bide our time. That we temper ourselves in all things. The card usually depicts a male pouring liquid from one glass to another. He isn't drinking, he is toying with that which might alter him. Instead of allowing alcohol or any other external factor to change his state of mind, he instead changes the state of things around him.

Often we allow the effects of substance and circumstance to push and pull us in and out of shape. We succumb to food, drink and experience easily. We feel we deserve particular options or rewards. We plan our day around how we can remove ourselves from the existence which we have become so bored with. We employ avoidance tactics and medicate against boredom, against life.

Temperance asks us to step into our plain life without the need to distract, reward, medicate or even meditate. Just to be. To be in this moment without filling it with anything else. Experience the void. Accept the void. Take it for what it is. See what occurs, what spirits rise, when the many intoxicating ghosts of consumer culture are halted.

MY JOURNEY

I am thinking that if you keep doing the same thing, and things never change, there should be no big surprise. Yet I keep doing the same things. To an extent. I improve with age. I learn, but some things remain the same. My reaction to my husband's depression is one of those things. I continually return to a raw and dark place. Yes, it might be diffused by my spirit animal, Elvis. But it sits in me heavy and weighted.

So I have revealed that darkest side of myself. From it I hope to arise to something different. I can only weigh my own soul. I am the only one whom I can find wanting. And I do, I find myself wanting that aspect of me to be gone.

When I look to my past I see that I entered into my marriage drunk, in Vegas. We never did do anything properly, husband and I. We just flowed with the moment. This has caught up with us. We have gone from young souls dancing through life, to older souls, tripping over the daily grit that most people are well practiced at by the time they are gliding towards 40. We have lost the flighty fun to the force that is family. I laugh with my daughters, but often forget to do so with my beloved.

There is this too: I can be cold. My life being charmed, and thus far free from any great trauma, has left me with an occasional lack of sympathy. That thing you are not supposed to say to depressed people, 'snap out of it'. I want to say that every time he gets down. I lack patience with it. I say I'm compassionate, but I could do better. This is part of my 'dirty', this is my glimmering filth.

Happily, today my husband has risen from his moody ashes. He was down for a couple of days. He has, over years, put the work in to make sure that his dark times are lessened: less frequent, less dark, less often. Yet my reaction to these dark patches, remains the same. I see that now. The symptoms have changed, but my inner medication has not. I have asked my husband to shift and to grow, and he has done so. Maybe I haven't? I'm sure I haven't. So I choose to experience a deep sense of grief every time he slips, irrespective of the depth of his slip. And yes, it is a choice.

I recently met a woman whose husband was depressed. She pins it all on him. Every disaster that befalls them, is down to him and the suffering he caused her. It occurred to me she couldn't fully see past her own suffering. She was so mired in it, in his lack, in her pain, that it never had a chance of improving for her. It had a tragic outcome. She took a very long time to overcome her part in this.

Occasionally she would drop in that her husband wasn't all bad, she would list his good points. But she left it at that, focusing instead on the less than flattering traits. I don't want to become her, making excuses for my life based on my husband's issues. I am my own woman. I am broiling in pain, when maybe, if I look at it objectively, with wisdom, I don't need to. I could take that pain and lessen it all by myself. I could see a bigger picture.

My pain is my habit, my addiction, the way I cope with things. But it doesn't work. I'm kidding myself if I believe that is has a purpose. Maybe once upon a time it did. We have moved past that day. I must start to see that. Only then can I embrace a future fused by my own being.

I don't want to write about this. I didn't want this to be what this book was about. This is my shadow side. I didn't want it illuminating. I forget that it is even there, and I like it that way. Because I am better than this. My fears, my worries, the fact that I entertain them at all, it feels deeply embarrassing. I'm British, we don't do weakness. I want none of this to be true. I don't want to look at it. I don't want you to look at it.

So that is where this journey is taking me. Precisely where I don't want to go. As I type this, 'Karma Police' by Radiohead is playing. This is my karma, neither bad nor good, just something that I get. This is what I get. I've given what I can, maybe I need to give differently. Maybe I need to break differently. My husband had a few down days, he was quiet. I wrote a book about it. Who has the bigger problem? That is the complexity of my feelings on the subject. What a trip: a shitty trip, a good trip, a trip to change all that I am.

There is nothing like a good toddler tantrum to shift you out of a self-imposed funk. My daughter, who seems to be embracing some massive life changes herself, had a lovely little tantrum this afternoon. It took all the strain right out of the air. My husband and I worked together, and all was nicely resolved. We worked together. We were cast onto the same team, and all that had consumed us left the room.

Temperance takes us forward. Slowly. Today my daughter represented the future, bringing us out of ourselves. Screeching us into the present, beating the dreary out of the air whilst donning a dragon costume and a bad attitude. I'm jolted into a new reality. One that is more important than all that has gone by. Built upon all of that, but not defined by it. Temperance, played through my daughter, as a portender of change. So I am back in the room.

HARNESS THE POWER OF TEMPERANCE.

Step back and look at the big picture of your life. Release the little things. See the passage of time as a chance to grow, rather than the ticking of a clock. Measure your life in improvement.

Place aside your usual crutches: television, booze, chocolate, magazines, long baths, yoga, gardening, the gym... Let go of rhythm and routine and just hang around yourself for the day.

DIRTY & DIVINE SPELLWORDS OF TEMPERANCE

I release what I have come to know, I grow from within.

15 – THE DEVIL

INTUITIVE MEANING

The Devil is the addiction you suffer under. The fear you labour beneath. All that keeps you meek and small can be attributed to this horned beast. He is not an evil entity keeping you in chains. He is you. He is the cold shudders that you answer with bad habits.

The Devil is chock full of fear for many tarot users. And yes, he isn't the nicest card to pull. But he only reflects those aspects of ourselves we push down and deny. Yet those aspects are never gone long. They raise up and enamour us to unhealthy ways of being. They bind us to fear. They create jails of self that can seem impossible to overcome. Not a human amongst us is free from the strong influence of The Devil. He is that moment of doubt, that internal worry, that regret, that hand reaching for a cigarette and that voice calling up to cancel.

His harm is only as real as you allow it to be. For whilst he lurks in your soul, he is not an embodied entity. He is not a spook that resides somewhere around your spine. He is simply you, disturbed, drained and dirty. Really fucking dirty.

MY JOURNEY

The Devil has me sweating and it's barely 7.30am. He is bringing me up against more truth. This time the type of truth that holds you in bondage to yourself. Since my eldest was born I've wanted to homeschool her. She has been my best little buddy, a soulmate, and I didn't plan to sever that connection with her by popping her into a red checked uniform and sending her off to school.

The bit holding me prisoner is that it is, for us, impractical, financially awkward and maybe not the best thing for me. I am stuck between a place of resenting my situation, but knowing on a practical level it makes a lot of sense. I'm trapped between my spiritual ideals and a cultural norm. Squidged awkwardly between the dirty and the divine.

This *Dirty & Divine* mission really is pitting my human self and my spirit up against one another and showing me the places where they rub. It's easy to let 'spiritual' beliefs, such as my desire to homeschool, become gritty and human. The ideal and fantasy of it has been railing against my reality for a while now. It is in moments like this, elucidated by the facts of the situation, where

I realise that what is causing me stress is my inability to budge past a four-year-old desire.

By making this situation about what I want, I engage The Devil. I wear blinkers. I can't see what is in front of me. I act for my joy and nobody else's. I spoke to my daughter for the first time ever about school today. She is so excited. I no longer need to be the gatekeeper to her safety. Well I do... But it's time to slacken the leash, to allow her to grow in a way that is right for her, whilst utilising a service provided for that purpose. Trusting all the while that this is the right thing, the perfect thing. Actively releasing those things that hold me tight and closed.

I guess that's my devilish theme for today. Letting go, releasing. A daughter is more tangible than a thought pattern or an addiction, though my love for her can fuel both those things. It is easy to allow our hopes to transmute into something unhealthy. My delirium over homeschooling, which started as a lovely possibility, has not moved with our times. So, instead, I will let go and trust. If I am meant to homeschool then I trust that this will become abundantly clear and possible. If I am not, then I have faith in the common path, in the village (it does purportedly take a village to raise a child). Either way, I consider the situation released.

The Devil always lies within. I'm not sure if I believe in exorcism or possession. I think that the demons are already within us, part of us, an essential part of our most gritty, human, primal self. How far into madness they send us depends on whether we capture and evade them sufficiently. I have seen people I love acting in a possessed manner, a grim darkness pouring forth from their eyes, anger, hate and misery emanating from their cells. These things were not the result of an external entity. They were that person's entity, twisted by addiction, exhaustion, fear, psychosis, sadness, perhaps a little madness. We all have it, and this is not meant to go any way to explain mental illness, but, perhaps there is something in that malady too, that seems otherworldly, but is otherwise our humanity, our dirty, expressing itself in wild, unkempt ways and fuelled by a barbed consciousness, awake, aware, thinking, and yet tainted by pain, overthought and a lack of self awareness. Our wilderness meets our modernity, meets substances, meets control and so internal havoc is invoked.

We are a people held captive by the structured society we live in. It is quite right that occasionally delirium of one sort or another takes over. Quite right indeed. Our maladies tell us who we should be. They are symptoms of boredom, stress, loneliness and dis-ease. These things are not innate devils, but the culturally created phenomena of living outside of nature, self and need. Instead we live in society, expectation and greed. As we lack our basic humanity, we become somewhat demonic, embracing anything that feels real, constantly missing the mark, yet howling to the skies, keening for purpose, love, meaning.

My Devil today was mild in comparison. But it still caused me pain. To reach inside and to recognise that the reason I was feeling sad and bad was my own doing: that is hard. Especially when I didn't want to change my heart and mind. I was happy stuck in my little rut. But since giving it to the goddess and the cosmos, my load has lightened. I have become acutely aware of my other child, my baby, who has for five months slept through most of life. Today she wants to play, watch cats and be with me. She was a beautiful surprise. She took us by storm. Now she's revamping my soul in directions anew. My children are angels to my devil, antidotes to the stress I inflict on myself, medicine to the wounds culture inflicts by forcing me to play along. Answers to the questions I didn't ask.

HARNESS THE POWER OF THE DEVIL

What is holding you back in your life? What is penning you in and limiting you? Pinpoint that aspect and choose to release it. Release expectation, release control, relinquish your hopes, desires and fears surrounding it. Drop your chains and choose to be free.

Clean and clear your space. As you do so imagine all that devilish energy being swept aside. Make a fresh start, literally.

Burn some incense, sage or palo santo to help rid your energies of darker vibes. Imagine them slipping from you. Give yourself permission to let them go.

DIRTY & DIVINE SPELLWORDS OF THE DEVIL

I am as free as I allow myself to be.

19 – THE SUN

INTUITIVE MEANING

Think all things sunny, all the clichés, poems, images and song lyrics collected and there you have the meaning of The Sun: bright, shining, a representation of god, life-giving. Everything grows under this light. If you are looking for divinity and Source, look no further. The Earth is our soil, our home, but without The Sun she would be barren. We are tag-teamed together to create life. One without the other is emptiness. We exist in a perfect dualism of happy accident, or lovely design. The Sun allows for us to see, to move, to be. He touches our dirt and up springs miracle.

Whilst The Sun is not necessarily depicted as male, I feel tempted to say that he is. The masculine is a beautiful thing. As a card-carrying feminist I forget that sometimes. I get so lost in railing against the patriarchy that I forget about all the really wonderful men, the fabulous male traits, the male inside of me. As much as men may get in touch with their inner woman, we too can benefit from radiating and glowing with our inner guy. The Sun is God. God is The Sun: benevolent, warming, joyful and life-giving.

MY JOURNEY

The sun has come out, quite literally. After the fog of winter, I am suddenly immersed in warm light. It is March and I am sat in the garden, sleeveless. The cats are sunbathing. My daughter is on my lap observing the outside world, properly, her first experience of it outside of a cot/sling/pram. She is supposed to be napping. But the sun is out, and who can blame her? The sky is blue. The sun is out!

I truly believe that life is reflected in all things, weather included. Today started with a literal thick fog. Whilst out driving I could only see about twenty feet ahead of me. Cars would loom out of nowhere, like approaching sharks in a sea boiling with sight-blurring salt. Something changed during the day and suddenly I realised that not only was the sun shining, but it was so warm. The light was bright and, just like a good Instagram filter, everything looked smooth, calm and divine.

Whilst my past few days have been a little roller coaster, The Sun figurative and literal has shown me that it was, to an extent, all in my head. I say I am one thing (a Tower) and then act another way (like someone falling out of a tower). I proclaim I am stable, but as soon as things look a little blue, I crack up. The sun is bringing spring and with that all those troubles, the internal nature of them, seems to be filtered out. I saw my dark side, and I did better. The sun helped. But of course he did.

And as I finished that paragraph, my head struck up with the Church of England school hymn classic of my youth, 'Shine baby shine, fill your heart with the Father's glory'. That's cool I'll take gods and goddesses right now. A little bit of all that is holy and sacred. Yes, thank you.

HARNESS THE POWER OF THE SUN

Be in the sun, let him touch your skin. Even in low sun, fog and storm, his light filters through. Seek it and absorb all it brings.

Consider your father figures. How have they illuminated your dark? If they haven't, expect better, wish for more, ask to be shown the divine male and find it, on the bus, at work, online or in your associates.

Get busy with your own inner masculine. Indulge some traditionally male habits or hobbies. Spend time with men you love and do what they like to do. Talk to your male people about what it is to be a man, then emulate that for a day. Ask your male aspects to engage and show you a little something.

DIRTY & DIVINE SPELLWORDS OF THE SUN

Together we grow.

20 – JUDGEMENT

INTUITIVE MEANING

Judgement, done so easily. Judgement, feared so badly. And yet, Judgement is but words and feelings compounded upon another, upon ourselves. It has meaning only in so far as we choose to believe it. But this is human judgement, and that will always find you wanting. Shame, guilt, fear and worry follow. In turn we judge another. As keen as we may be not to be judgemental, it happens. We rein it in, and then damn those opinions nudge at our surface just longing to be given air.

Divine judgement is something altogether different. Judgement is the card that reflects our coming together with our higher self. Merging with all that we are, free from taint, sin and dirt. Forgiven perhaps. It reflects the meeting of our body with our soul. It provides healing that leads to a new dawn and full movement away from the past.

Judgement is not justice. It is the inevitability of karma. It is the ferocious meeting of your own soul and the human you have become. From here you can move closer to your own personal source. Or you don't. Spiritual, divine, sacred judgement leads to redemption and forgiveness, eventually, always, in this life, or perhaps, the next.

MY JOURNEY

Do I feel redeemed and worthy? I'm not sure if any of us ever can. I struggle with this card in readings because it is just so big. It's life and death, heaven and hell. It is dirty and divine. How do you apply those themes to a life without coming up short?

I guess that little crystals of judgement inflict themselves into our lives every day. Every ending, every realisation, every movement forward contains fractions of what it means to live, to die and mostly to grow. This *Dirty & Divine* journey has pulled me up against myself. I hope that those things I have sought to change and heal, are allowing for me to be set free, to be judged and found a little more divine.

Who is this judging me? Well, myself of course. Myself as I sit here, and my higher self, the self of me that exists beyond the borders of flesh. The spiritual me. Though, I suspect, she is less judgemental. Perhaps I am only presuming her judgement. Maybe I shouldn't speak on her behalf. The real judge here is the very much incarnate me.

It's a never-ending trip, though. One set of circumstances replaces another and we work our way through it, hopefully coming off better, bolder versions of ourselves, eventually. As I lay waste to certain parts of 'me', other aspects arise. In time new issues crop up, and I take the opportunity, if I am wise, to fix those issues with love, spirit and faith.

Judgement is a card of review. In reviewing my passage through each card I have been challenged. Its timing is perfect, because from here, the next card is The World. So today I assess my journey, see what I've learned, hold it close to my heart and commit to making it mean something. I can feel redeemed and worthy, for now, until the next dirty jumps out from within. I prepare to squiggle closer to my divine, my purpose, my truth. Tomorrow, The World looms.

HARNESS THE POWER OF JUDGEMENT

Review your *Dirty & Divine* journey so far. Where has it taken you? What have you learned?

Prepare within for a new world, the calling of your soul, using the past as a diving board. Breathe deeply, assimilate your lessons, know that change is afoot, and plunge headlong.

DIRTY & DIVINE SPELLWORDS OF JUDGEMENT

I forgive, release, and journey past my judgement.

21 – THE WORLD

INTUITIVE MEANING

Another celestial body, but one that we know, that we touch, that is our home. It is easy to look to the sky for our mystery, our magic. And yet here we are atop a spinning ball of stardust, one that is teeming with the most fascinating life. What is more incredible: a ball of rock in the sky, gifting us gravity and hormonal pull? Or a lush blue and green landscape that we can touch, influence and be consciously within. It's easy to go searching for something 'more', presuming the grass is greener in a far flung galaxy. Yet we have our own grass, so much of it, on our little Gaia, our loving Mother Earth.

The World represents possibility, opportunity, growth and change. She is spirited in all her ways: a living, energetic and intelligent being. We are aspects of her, birthed from within her soils, living solely with her agreement. We can choose to co-create alongside her, bringing forth our spirit to her physical realm. We may not realise it, but we can be aligned and in sync with her magic. When we step into her nature, her flow, anything, anything, anything is possible.

The World is always turning. This card represents the completion of a part of your life. You have sailed successfully to a new port, a new place to begin the next adventure. The dance of life begins anew.

MY JOURNEY

Well, I have certainly danced my way through some turmoil this past Major Arcana month. I've raised my demons and inner conflicts and sent them spiralling away from me. I feel like I have successfully released the past that was dogging me. It feels very much like a new start, another chance, a moment of beginning.

So today I am to expect The World. Which sounds rather grand. But of course The World shows up in many shades. It is clipping your toenails, it is amazing sex, it is the Maldives, it is Fukushima. The World is all and whatever we want it to be. The stage is set, but whether we follow the lines, or improvise, is down to us.

I have no words of wisdom on whether it is better to stay within or without of the box. I believe all life has purpose. Small lives matter. Big lives matter. Each of us can affect thousands through how we conduct ourselves. Society's version of The World expects big achievements to be seen as worthy. This is a popularity competition on an unhealthy scale.

Life, love and importance are not weighed soulfully on the same scale that mass culture measures. Do the people who mean most to you harbour Oscars, Nobel prizes and millions of dollars in their bank accounts? Or do they possess some other less tangible skills and assets? Those that do have awards and certificates stacking up, do you love them for that, or in spite of that? Success is no real measure of anything in this world. 'It's the heart that matters more' just poured into my head, courtesy of The Counting Crows. You don't need to be anything or anyone or be anywhere, what The World, the true World, cares about is your heart.

So where is your heart at? Last night I had a little cry. So very unlike me. This journey through the Major Arcana has shuffled my bones. I had a cry about all that I am letting go of: ingrained beliefs and dusty desires. My husband talked me back round, echoing my reasoning, reminding me that I need to let go a little. It's hard, and I needed to grieve it, so a little spilt mascara helped chug that process along.

Sometimes the heart is so full of love that we want to keep that love penned up, for fear of it spilling out and away. The World, the divine, the sacred feminine ask us to open the floodgates and perceive the opportunity of that love growing, expanding and multiplying. Go forth and multiply, motherfuckers.

I have learned these past few days that putting a fence around love simply allows fear to grow up the sides of it like creeping virginia. It roots around, into cracks, making us tight and unyielding. Removing those fences is scary at first, but opening to the potential for great joy is exciting. We are not meant to live in a little vacuum, reserving love for those we have married, spawned or met via Facebook. We must open our hearts to the divinity of our love. Shower it upon those we meet. Practise what you preach, Alice, practise what you preach.

Today we went to visit an elderly relative: my husband's grandma. She is chuntering glamorously close to one hundred years old and is the sweetest lady. She is a modern crone, made-up perfectly in a thick coat of Max Factor, hair dyed black, with more great grandchildren than she can count. She is a real wonder. She has borne five children and mourned the death of two, alongside her beloved husband too.

This is the other end of life. Doreen has never known the stark ambition we have. Her loves were her children, her life, her own mother. You want the divine feminine, in its rawest sense? Here it is. Unsullied by any spiritual perspective, she just is: Mother Earth. Simple, devoted to her immediate situation, fully embodied within it, to this day wearing the bracelets given to her by each child, lamenting the opportunity to have had more and repeatedly wondering how people could hurt children. She told us that if she had her time again she would work in a children's home, and if she sensed one of the children wasn't loved (because she has heard of that happening) ooohhhh, she would love that child. By golly she would!

What a dame! None of this is to say that one must be a mother to experience the divine feminine. Not at all. But to live embodied by love, for all beings, is a good place to start looking. To be a mother to our work, our garden, our own inner child, our cats, our friends, our self, our day. Because this is where life begins, so humble, so infused with something effervescent and transcendent. Something that simply will not be shunted even from a fading memory.

The world is missing such love. The divine feminine, so squashed and bent out of shape, is missing. Put all else aside: your lust for renown, your hope for a holiday, your ambition, your personal hopes, your self-help. Perhaps it could all be a little answered when filtered through that sprightly unconditional love. You have this within you, your divine feminine, your pure love. Allow it to rise, to infiltrate your senses and to bring you home.

HARNESS THE POWER OF THE WORLD

Centre your thoughts on those things you love, not the things you want, but the people, places and powers that are already yours. Act with these as your centre.

Connect to Mother Earth. Take a few moments to notice something new outdoors. Look up, see the clouds drifting by, bringing beauty, shelter, rain and storms. Look down, see the weeds sprouting through concrete. Notice the power of this planet as she gently invades our human constructions.

DIRTY & DIVINE SPELLWORDS OF THE WORLD

I am The World.

MAJOR ARCANA REVIEW

This first part of the trip, journeying through the Major Arcana, has been a blast. Or more like an explosion. All that wanted airing from within me, those things rotting at my core certainly took this opportunity to fling themselves to the surface. At the same time, mystery and wisdom floated their way through the festering filth and became explanation and story to my journey. It's been far more eye-opening than I expected. I hope that you have found these archetypes have brought you into close consideration of your dirty and your divine. Repeating this exercise every few years would be a powerful tool upon which a healthy soul can turn.

MINOR ARCANA

So for now we are leaving the Major Arcana behind and moving on to the Minor Arcana. The Minor Arcana are the sand between our toes. Oftentimes insignificant, and yet at other times the irritants that, when stimulated, change lives. Thus far our journey has been big. It's been big themes, big inner issues, big changes. The Minor Arcana are perfectly capable of creating more of the same. They may also whittle down our concentration to the smaller aspects of self that need a tickle.

I'm particularly interested in how the Minor Arcana, which naturally fall into themed groups, will create or tell a story about our lives. Each Major Arcana card is a play unto itself. Whereas the Minors are a progression into an understanding of each theme; I'm expecting intrigue.

Whilst the stories may be smaller, the images and meaning of the cards can be so powerful. The Minor cards are open to interpretation in the way that the Major may not be. The picture sat astride the card can mean so many different things, dependent on the mood and details of your life at any given time. The fact that the images are somewhat less striking allows them to be more fluid. Though, of course, that too is down to personal interpretation.

As you journey through the Minor cards, allow their individual intrigue to emerge. If you ever get stuck on the meaning of a card, if it is being elusive, then maybe try pulling a second card, one to help frame and reflect it. As I always say, the interpretation, in the end, is always yours. What your heart is saying, the words that float up, these are the right ones. Move into trust that what you feel, think and understand as you gaze upon any card, is what is right for you. Feel free to bounce off friends who are on this same journey, but know that their guidance is a pointer only. Your truth, your feeling, that is where the depth and learning is at.

As for the theme of each suit. It is there, and yet it is not. For example, the Cups are related to emotion and love. But this does not mean that your story, for the duration of the Cups, will be a love story. Be open to what the cards bring. As you journey through them, you will be gifted insight: surprising, flammable, always unforeseen insight. There is no point having expectations, these will be blown to dust. I will give you a directional theme at the start of each suit. Please tuck it in your top pocket and forget about it.

You may wonder: why bother continuing, when what we have already explored was so significant? I wonder the same. I'm in this with you. So rather than wonder, or worse, not even bother, let's continue onward. Let us set our intent to wonder and revelation, with a side dose of marvel and travel forward.

THE CUPS

Here we begin with love. We ended the Major Arcana on that same feeling, so let us continue.

The Cups represent emotion, relationships, family, friends and all that makes us emotive, feeling creatures. Consider yourself a vessel. What do you contain? What guides your day? You contain, you hold, you are a receptacle of feeling. This feeling is the seat of much of our longing and learning. It informs all. Each card projects us through the kaleidoscope of all of that, bringing us up to our multifaceted ability to exist in a state of being with others.

The Cups are associated with water. The feminine comes through the Cups powerfully. We women are (often) so damned good at feeling. Feeling is something we have been allowed to do, even if we have in turn been mocked and derided for it. There may be tears, deep feelings and memories surfacing as this part of the journey continues. Perhaps years of feeling will see that this part of your journey is dry eyed and theoretical. There will likely be feelings about feelings. All that has ever been loved by you, and all that might ever be loved by you, is set to shine in your mind.

ACE OF CUPS

INTUITIVE MEANING

A fresh abundant start is arising. Each Ace card of every suit tends to offer new beginnings, new energy. In the Ace of Cups, we see a passage, a potential for a new emotionally wise and abundant path. Abundance being based in happiness, rather than the commercial glimmer of money and possessions. You hold the key to making wonderful things happen, to understanding just what is wonderful. Sometimes we must recognise the value of what we already have, so that we can be the abundant recipient of more of the same. Expect goodness to grow and love to expand, and only then, they will.

MY JOURNEY

The spin of my world has been internal. The routine continues. But inwardly so much has changed. The Ace of Cups adds a new slant to my love, my life and my perspective.

This is just the beginning of a new way of being. Love is palpable and will surely be a guiding light.

I found myself asking my husband to be a house-husband today. Requiring me to be the main breadwinner. Not quite what I expected from myself, seeing as I dream of being. . .

That last sentence was interrupted by myself and my husband having a huge argument. We don't do shouting and yelling. We do frustrated bickering and then dozens of text messages around the house, back and forth, venting and yelling using text as opposed to vocals.

Fuck. The entire context of the day changed, just like that. From divine to dirty in the sweep of one bad mood. I'm not even entirely sure what that was all about. I know he called me bossy and I know I called him Cinderella. Perhaps this house-husband idea was not the best I've ever conceived.

I'm not sure how this is the beginning that I was just lauding. It doesn't feel like one. It feels irksome and vapid and pointless. Gritty, shitty and dirty. My only hope is that from chaos good things do come. I know that they do. So I will wait and hope that this little molehill ushers up some good.

HARNESS THE POWER OF ACE OF CUPS

Whatever situation you find yourself in, take it for what it is. All things can be new starts. The old can be a catalyst. The miserable can be a personal moon landing. Fresh starts don't always show up wrapped in spotless cellophane with trumpets declaring their arrival. New starts can be small, unnoticed motes of dust, floating in on an unknown breeze. See what today brings and assume that it is some crack of an opening into something else.

DIRTY *&* DIVINE SPELLWORDS OF ACE OF CUPS

I allow what comes.

TWO OF CUPS

INTUITIVE MEANING

Partnership, lovers, soulmates maybe even. This card represents two people who work together, who fit, who offer themselves to the other, and together they are stronger. It is a little like The Lovers, but more grounded and earthy, it is more realistic. It is not borne out of hedonistic pleasure, but taken and grown from the bowels of being, true, grim and graceful being.

MY JOURNEY

I woke to my husband ringing me, not for the usual apology, but for the lesser opted, 'I'm an alcoholic and I'm going to AA' telephone call. This happens every once in a while. He is an addict of some description. Something to which I am often in denial. The trip through the Major Arcana contained elements of addiction, but I edited them out, because he isn't a roaring drunk, he isn't abusive, he doesn't even smell of booze. It is undetectable. Except for the weird mood he gets into, the arguments over nothing, the blame he places outside of himself: on me, his parents, his work. Maybe it is problem drinking, maybe it's the wrong side of a bad habit. Maybe this is all just words. The fact is, there is some sort of something.

It's time we showed up to the truth, both of us. Just because he isn't tripping over his tongue or his feet, does not put him in the clear. The repeated cycle of his drinking and its effects on us, gnawing at the heart of our home, is very real.

I spent the morning dazed, ready to leap on the next bus to Divorceville — as is my habit. From the fire to the frying pan. I did the sums. I Googled separation agreements. I gave up on him, quite significantly. How many more times do we suffer, get to this point and then slowly decline back towards this same moment, several weeks from now? Over and over. Till death do us part...

So I stepped into my truth and we spoke, not texted, spoke. He wants to beat it; he wants my support. I tell him that my support makes him comfy, tricks him into that first drink, because on paper he has it all: a home, a wife, kids, a job. The slide begins through my support. I'm his enabler. Despite every cell in my soul wanting him to recover, I somehow become a blankie that makes it all go away and just one drink seem reasonable... Just the one...

Things need to be different this time. Something has to be different. It cannot be the same. I came back down from my divorce bubble. I aimed towards love. This time though I am setting boundaries, I'm asking him to agree to a strict schedule of

AA visits and full disclosure to all friends and family. He said he was going to put it on Facebook. Maybe that will help. For me, so far, it looks like I'm talking to you about it.

I'm not going to talk about this much more for the fear that this book will turn into tarot marriage counselling by proxy. What I will say, that is relevant to us all is this: the tarot know you. I set out on this journey in the full awareness that shit might arise. I secretly hoped for wonderful things to pop up, ya know, like Beyoncé retweeting me and sending my writing world stellar, that kind of simple nonsense.

What I have learned is that you cannot hide from the tarot, from the crack of your bones. In this aspect there is something quite occult about them indeed. They see through you. In this instance they forced me to see the obvious problem, camouflaged by daily life, but dying for a resolution. Even today, on the Two of Cups, we see two lovers in a face off. I never saw this card like that before. I saw it as a union, soulmates and the Disney version of all that is love. I have been brainwashed. I wanted a prince. I got us. I don't want to be a fucking princess. I see that today those two partners are not in a place of fairy-tale joy, but in a space whereby they must offer each other their deepest honesty to be able to move forward. There may be a happy-ever-after, there may well, but for now all we have is gut-wrenching grit and a table upon which to place it.

HARNESS THE POWER OF TWO OF CUPS

What are you bringing to the table of your relationships?

Where could you bring more truth? Apply this to friendships, lovers and family.

DIRTY & DIVINE SPELLWORDS OF TWO OF CUPS

I get what I give.

THREE OF CUPS

INTUITIVE MEANING

Call your goddess friends. This card is all that is female power. It is the Holy Trinity. I'm not talking martyrs, spirits and heavenly dads. I'm talking you and your best other two women, whomever they may be: dancing, chatting, being. The Holy Trinity, the threesome, your three best witches, the fucking coven.

It is whatever you do to reconnect to the women in your life. If you rock climb, do that. If you dance and drink, do that. If you chat over tea and biscuits, do that. If you do lunch, then do lunch. Be with women who make you shine, who put things in perspective, who make you more yourself.

MY JOURNEY

What a blessed relief. Some female relief, to take over my burdens of the past few days. Just momentarily contemplating the memories I have of such wonderful women has proven to be soul food. Indeed, as the day has gone by I have been gifted with wonderful glimpses of friendship from those I know not quite so well also.

I have always been in friendship groups of three. Whilst no Wiccan purpose underlined this, it is a powerful number. It is the number given to God and his pals by mainstream religion. It is the number Shakespeare gave to his awesome hags at the start of Macbeth. It is the number of witches cast together to form a meaningful coven. It is the Trinity. The Pyramid. Representative of higher power, higher self, the illuminati. Your illuminati.

I have experienced so much of life through my female triads. I can't even begin to express the richness these female threesomes have brought to me. It seems implausible that we ever ended up shacking up with dudes, because the best stuff, the funniest stuff, the deep down soul bearing stuff is reserved for my gal pals. Doubtless.

Of course I have friendships that started as a three and then became less. I also have singular friends, or groups of friends. Of course now I am in a very permanent three-way of me and my two daughters. I really don't know what the thing is about this. I just know it is a thing, a lovely thing. When I sleep I don't dream of ex-boyfriends or male associates. I dream of female friends gone past. They are there, vivid as they ever were, adventuring with me through the dozing hours.

The fact that so many formative and supportive friendships, for me, have come as a threesome is an intrigue. Particularly as three is allegedly a crowd. Like a perfect coven of witches, so much has been set right over bottles of wine, good dinners, tarot cards and the occasional spa date. Gosh that sounds girly. But I am a girl, I love my girls, I'm damned girly. And it is within this girliness that so much divinity pours forth.

There is a reason why we attest to not being 'girly'. It's because we don't want to be stereotyped as some kind of Barbie by the world at large. We spurn pink, in favour of blue, and that is our activism for the day. What I believe nowadays though, is that the ultra-anti-girliness stance that can be taken, is as anti-feminist as anything else. Because girls are awesome. Yes, it may seem impolite to label a grown woman a 'girl', but then my query is, what is wrong with being a girl? Why are we so damned tied up with maturity, that being a girl is a bad thing? And what is wrong with pink? The fact it is related to the feminine, somehow renders it less than, and therefore worthy of rebuke. If we reject pink, we reject aspects of the feminine. Why not instead, grasp those aspects, the 'girliness', and own it. Not in the way it is currently sold to us, but in a new way. In a, my vagina is pink, my tongue is pink, my womb is pink, my heart is pink, kinda way. It's not a part of the oppression unless we concede that the pink heart of us is worthy of oppressing.

Worryingly though anything feminine is liable to be found wanting. That's just the way it has been for a long, long time. Playing into this by adorning or abhorring all that is girly, is beside the point. We should be free to be whatever we want, in whatever shade we like and under any circumstances in all venues.

So today I am thinking on my friendships and finding myself all warm and cosy. These memories are not of colour or some kind of girl code. They are full of depth, philosophy, wilderness and a fair share of red wine. The women I know are a spectrum of all human life. The only one I can think of who comes close to being a pinkie, is, in fact, probably me. That, I believe, is based upon my teenage rebellion against the radical feminism I was raised in. That type of feminism was powerful, but from my perspective sometimes hypocritical, and a little scary. That's humanity, though, isn't it? Hypocritical to the hilt, deep down scary. Hypocrisy goes with the territory. Look at me: divine one minute, dirty the next.

Today I attended a Kids Club with my daughters. It is run by a mother and daughter. It's just a Kids Club. But at the same time it's an awesome gaggle of women becoming slowly bonded over children and babies and cups of tea. Today was the last ever group. It was ending due to issues of space. They made such a fuss over the children, and the mothers. It was so lovely.

People don't expect to be treated as special. That's the deal these days. You are only special if you are paying for something. The best salespeople make you feel fabulous, but it generally costs something. It's very rare that you are made a fuss over for nothing, and for no reason.

I can only guess at the reason why these two lovely women ran the Kids Club. I know why they were good at it. Because they must have loved it. What they did made a difference. It wasn't just a generic club, it was special. They made it special. That was their choice and doing. I believe that power is inferred by plain old love. Love of kids, love of playing, love of doing something for people.

This is why I love women, and my wonderful girlfriends. Because they make you feel special, at no cost and with no agenda. It just is. Friendship for its own sake is such a gift.

I saw one of my best women friends today. She is part of a triad that has not been together as a threesome for quite some time. Our hay days were in our mid-twenties, shot-fuelled and preferably taken in the local rock club. We had fun. We found dirty and we revelled in it.

We sobered up, got married, had kids all within years of each other. Now she and I are trying to carve out paths for ourselves in life, in business, trying to live on purpose. I love that our existences seem to echo one another's so acutely. I love that she gets where I am at without even having to hardly say a word. I feel her.

There is something in this female friendship. It's divine. But not just because it makes us happy. It's deeper than that. It is often here that we glow with intuition. With our male mates, our boyfriends, our husbands and brothers we may come up with a blank. Yet with our fellow females, we just have a knowing, and understanding, a way of getting each other that surpasses body language and the verbal. It is innate, it is of this planet and yet it is out of this world. We take it for granted. We laugh it off as women's intuition. We giggle that our periods have synced and that we knew which friend was calling as soon as we heard that first ring.

It's not funny though. Nor is it a coincidence. Our women are the platform upon which our spirituality begins to arise, our deep powerful souls start to show themselves. Yes, it may occur over something as vapid as matching nails and shoes. Yes, it may announce itself in a high pitched 'I was just thinking that same thing'. These are just the tip of the iceberg. We are shaman wild women consorting over cocktails. Imagine if we took it deeper. Imagine if we got psychic and intuitive and tuned into each other on purpose. Holy fuck, no wonder society oppresses and separates us.

I don't know what might occur if many women chose to get together in loving harmony to take things deeper. I'm curious. I see the start of a new women's spiritual movement arising and I feel like we are on the verge of something perhaps more pioneering and powerful than any radical feminist (any human even) might imagine or dream.

Women being together without a plot or a plan. Just to support and inspire one another. Just to see what happens and to just be in the moment. To celebrate the fact we are all female. To be in awe of each other. To give ourselves what society refuses to give: credit, appreciation, understanding. There is potential here, and it drives through politics, culture and even spirituality. This is it. This could be the New World Order. Sign me up.

All the gritty, shitty blah I have been dealing with at home with the man. It's all good, it's learning, I love him, this is my life. But I am on fire for the women right now. The healing and spiritual communion my soul needs right now is very much from the ladies. Today has shown me that. The passion I have felt flare in me as I contemplate the friendships with the people of my own gender, the goddesses, the divine feminine of the lasses around me has been spectacular. I'm bordering on lesbian right now. Though it's not about the sex, not for me. I want them for their minds, and their souls. I want the Women. I want them now.

HARNESS THE POWER OF THREE OF CUPS

Get with the girls. Call them, be with them, think of them.

DIRTY & DIVINE SPELLWORDS OF THREE OF CUPS

Power to my women.

FOUR OF CUPS

INTUITIVE MEANING

Feeling ambivalent towards one's blessings. Meditating and perhaps mediating on choice. Becoming serious and sullen whilst trying to control life. Not recognising the freedom and gifts of an alternative.

Get out of your head and into your heart.

MY JOURNEY

'You do it to yourself, you do, and that's what really hurts.'
Radiohead

I'm doing it again. I'm rehashing possibilities and getting nowhere. It's the old school/homeschool saga again. I just spent twenty minutes planning to devise some propaganda in support of delayed schooling. I was convinced that given the right evidence I could bring my husband round to my way of thinking. I was literally going to make him sit down and I was going to do a presentation. I had it all worked out.

I was reading through the evidence and feeling exasperated because I realised it was not actually convincing me. It was a wishy-washy attempt to vie for something halfway between what we think we want. I tried to align myself with that, rather than continue to entertain the inner turmoil, the old hopes, the desires of her babyhood.

Four of Cups has me banged to rights. It has seen my prevarication and called me on it. So what am I failing to see? I think I'm failing to see my own intuition on this. I'm so torn between a hope and what might be easier. A desire and a convenience.

It's aggravating to have two sets of ideas flying around one's head and not quite knowing which one will define your life. It's the age-old problem of thinking that our mind can fix anything at all. Indeed, the assumption that there is anything to fix, is something that is negotiable. I ought really just let it go again. That's what I must do.

I think I need to give myself a break from all of this and breathe. Who knows, when I look away from this, what might arise. I wrote the word 'homeschool' down on some paper, and I burned it. I ask the divine feminine, the goddess to remove my fear and help give me clear sight, align me with my intuition and to carry this forward for the highest purpose of everyone.

HARNESS THE POWER OF FOUR OF CUPS.

What situation is your mind tackling and fixating on? Make efforts to let it go. Choose to let it go. Write it down on some paper and burn it. Let. It. Go. Allow what is awaiting your attention to come forward.

Allow the flow of life to bring you a solution today. Don't try to create one. Simply expect one instead. Think no more on it and see where this takes you.

DIRTY *&* DIVINE SPELLWORDS OF FOUR OF CUPS

I release my need to be in control. I allow all that I deserve.

FIVE OF CUPS

INTUITIVE MEANING

The Five of Cups reflects the ease with which we can get lost in the drama and chaos of the past. In doing so, we miss the gifts we have already and the beauty yet to come. Indeed, we too easily forget how all that drama of the past helped cause the blessings we are currently ignoring.

MY JOURNEY

It's pretty hard to navigate life without continual reference to what came before. That, I feel, is reasonable. It's when the past takes a hold of our senses that we have problems. When we swerve off course, due to a fear or pattern ingrained from prior years, that's not healthy. If we choose to actively close down possibility, due to things which happened previously, that's a problem. Or when we get so mired in the drama of life as it was, what hurt us, what somebody said or did, or how things have been unfair and cruel, that's just asking for more of the same. We then receive more of the same as evidence of what it was we first learned and nothing ever changes.

In short, the past is useful as a frame of reference and a box out of which we can break. It isn't, however, a mould. We can scribble outside of previous lines. We can look up from the script and see a new actor, a new stage, a new set, a whole new us on the periphery, just waiting for us to jump into role.

Once upon a time I was a blonde Swedish nanny involved in a rather complicated sex farce with two middle aged married couples. It was a comedic play based out of the city's amateur dramatic theatre. I loved it and I hated it. In the middle of the week I forgot one of my lines and felt traumatised ever after. It's not something I think about now. Though it is something I dream about. I dream about being in a play and knowing I have to go on stage and that I don't know any of my lines. A classic anxiety dream that perhaps points to my worries over my role in life.

The other night I had the same dream, except this time I wasn't scared, I was excited. I knew I could easily learn the lines and, if all else failed, I would improvise. The past is not a prison. We can make it up as we go along. We should make it up as we go along.

I believe that this *Dirty & Divine* journey is the cause of my dream changing. I am being shaken hard and the toxic elements are rearing up, then falling away as I actively address them. It is all based on the past, it has to be. It is the past that informs so much. We cannot, however, look forward with it as a guide. As a memory, yes, but a guide, no. There are no roadmaps made successfully from memory. The compass we truly need resides within and bubbles up via the faith we choose to have.

HARNESS THE POWER OF FIVE OF CUPS

Look to the future. Without expectation. Know that as you shift away from the past new ways of being and understanding your role in this life will appear.

If the past arises and begs you to feel it, turn away. Look elsewhere. Seek the present and all that is valuable within it.

DIRTY & DIVINE SPELLWORDS OF FIVE OF CUPS

I am not what I was.

SIX OF CUPS

INTUITIVE MEANING

The inner child is calling, asking you to connect to innocence, simple joy and full self-knowing. This card asks you to reflect on your younger years: what guidance might be found within the realm of your childhood? What aspects of self did you leave behind that might be rising again? Do not dwell in a longing for simpler times, but rather bring the simplicity to your present door, welcome it in, bake it a sticky cake and play hide and seek. Only this time be sure not to let your little self get lost forever. Keep her close.

MY JOURNEY

I look at adults my age, younger sometimes, and I wonder when they became so grown up? How did they lose that spark of youth quite so dramatically? Where did it go? What has been left afterwards, other than responsibility and wine?

I just don't feel quite grown up yet. That's a lie. Until recently I didn't feel grown up. Then I had a second child and I feel now like I'm moving toward being an older woman. Not grown up. But older, wiser and strangely excited to wear my wrinkles with wisdom and wit. Just today a gentleman said 'excuse me young lady'. I ignored him because I couldn't conceive that he was speaking to me.

I don't believe in being grown up. I feel it's an untruth. It's something that keeps us bored and orderly. The reality is that we are little, then we are big, and eventually we accumulate the knowledge we had deep down anyway. If we are lucky we return to being the person we were before the world worked it out of us. If we are lucky.

Childhood. That's a weird one too. These days I see kids as wise little beings with wild temperaments and so much love. Their bodies are too little to contain all that they are and so their energy, thoughts and feelings are played out rambunctiously. I'm a very easy-going parent, probably quite permissive. That's because I believe that my children are souls separated from me only by a tiny fragment of experience. I guide them and steer them and keep them safe and warm and loved. Beyond that, I'm not their zoo keeper. They are my brood, not my caged birds.

I look to my little girl self and again I find I am astonished. I was a cute kid. I had no conception of that. I was a sweet kid, mostly. Again I didn't really have an understanding of that either. Kids are an etheric mess. They show up in a body and to begin with their idea of self is negligible. Once the labels start this alters and forever influences who they believe they are. But prior to that there is space of existence where kids are everything. All at once. They don't exist as an individual entity. Until the day that they do.

Here lies the innocence I'm looking for. Not the innocence before we learned about sex and death, but the innocence of not even being quite aware of your own self. There is a powerhouse there. Something quite unique to be brought into our adult understanding of self. The fact that we can be creatures of simplicity. That we are at one with all. That we can live wholly on trust and faith.

I just nipped out to the local supermarket and nursed my daughter in the cafe. As we were relaxing together the song 'Return to Innocence' came on. Half an hour later it's still swimming round my mind and I've only just clocked the connection.

Innocence, like cuteness or sweetness, is not really a thing. It can't be lost because it's just a word, a concept and an idea. Your innocence wasn't taken; you didn't give it away. It isn't a bargaining chip. Innocence is simply the expansion of self to a much bigger picture. It is becoming peaceful within and offering love and joy out. If we step back from our ego and the labels applied to us we can view our lives as an energetic puzzle piece.

We fit into a world that tests us and that also makes perfect space for us. We ripple out through our actions and others ripple across us. Innocence is the fragment of soulful spark that sits within us as we surf those tides. It is always there. You may be closest to it at either extreme of age. You are closest to it when you allow yourself to be. You are closest to it when you lay down your arms and release your defences.

Innocence arises in vulnerability and in bliss. Sex is lauded by many as the loss of innocence. But that is just patriarchal prudishness talking. That just gives weight to all those sexist labels and to the idea that 'sexy' is wholly dirty. Sex is another way into innocence, into your core, into connection and communion with another through a transcendental physical, energetic, sometimes spiritual experience. That's something women have to fight for. For sex to be more than a physical pornographic experience. For it to be meaningful. For it to be innocent and pure. We have to fight to raise it from the dirt, the filth it has been mired in. Because it can be.

The fact it is deemed otherwise says more about men than it does about women. Because they are the ones who allegedly defile us. They must have such low opinions of themselves, such embarrassment about their own sexuality. If the dirt starts with them, and we are the recipients of it, who really, at heart believes themselves to be lesser? That is the thing. We hate others for what we see in ourselves, and what we fear we are not. So taken like that we may see that sexual patriarchy is simply a reaction to the purity men desire and the fear of their own filth. All projected powerfully and cruelly upon the feminine.

Here is a thought: when does a man lose his innocence by societal standards? Never. Because he isn't endowed with the mythic qualities of the innocent. But he, like us, is a spark of spirit. I feel bad for men here. Cultural talk on guys suggest they are wrong. The spectrum of male sexuality ranges from horny and lusty to pervy and rapey. Guys are societally gross; their sex drive is consistently subject to ridicule. We get the choice of good or bad girl. They just get grimy, gritty and the continued myth that their bollocks talk louder than their brains. Their desires are made filth, made funny, made fractious. There is little room or reality for them either. The dialogue around sex does nobody any good, does it?

I fear that this is another attempt by a patriarchal society to do us all out of our power. We are repelled from the most intimate act by way of language that strips the spirit from sex. The only ones benefitting from our wiles, are the men, who we are actively taught to seek out from girlhood. It all plays nicely into the hands of a society stacked in the favour of the penis. And that penis has a life of his own: unknown to his owner, lost in expectation, presumption and parody.

This just refers to heterosexuality. The perspective of lack of innocence when it comes to other sexualities gets even more base. The common factor is that sex, decided to be the loss of some kind of purity, is made fearful. Men are scary because they are lustful, abandoned and violent. Women are scary because they are needy, consuming and may taint you with their lack. Gay people are scary because their sexuality is warped, unnatural and deluded. Trans people are scary because it may all be a trick just to assault you in a bathroom. Bisexual people are puerile, attention-seeking hippies who want to challenge the norm.

Think about when animals fuck: they do it and move on. There is no meal made of it. No judgement. A moment of copulation and then onwards. As deeply sentient beings we choose to add layers to the sexual experience. We could make those layers pretty, joyful and loving. Somewhere those layers became ugly, furious and tainted.

Yet the thing is, perhaps, maybe, just imagine if, sexuality is one of the purest things we have. One of the most innocent things we have. To experience pleasure, alone or alongside another, or others, together, in vulnerability, experiencing something exquisite. That's pure, surely? That is innocent. Even if it gets a little gorgeously twisted. If you enjoy your physical being, then that's a little essential something right there. It's the ultimate escape, the purest form of being, in self, in being, for your innocence. Forget meditation. Forget forty days of fasting. Forget your self-denial. Go straight for the bone. Fuck, be fucked, fuck a little, fuck a lot. Fuck with desire, heart, love, lust, need, greed. Make the fucking something other than the cultural fantasy it has become. Whatever it is, whatever it becomes, if it is consenting, if it feels good, decide it to be pure. Decide yourself to be pure.

HARNESS THE POWER OF SIX OF CUPS

Consider yourself redeemed, healed, forgiven and pure. No goddess of mine holds a grudge. You are an innocent. Live with that in your heart, your head, your hair and your pants for the day.

DIRTY *&* DIVINE SPELLWORDS OF SIX OF CUPS

I reclaim my innocence.

SEVEN OF CUPS

INTUITIVE MEANING

Choice, confusion, delusion. Is what you are being offered quite as it seems? Which road do you take? Mystification, confusion, uncertainty. A fog has descended and you can't figure a way through. Maybe that is perfect. Stew in the fog a while, embrace it, allow for the possibility of change and guidance to come to you.

MY JOURNEY

I awoke to tiredness, as was expected. Both my girls are sick again with colds. My eldest is currently suffering a cold in her eyes. Yes, it is as mucus-y and swollen as it sounds. I awoke to her at 1am with puddles of gunk in and around her eyes. The baby then woke and decided she had a bit of a cold too and needed snot sucking out of her nose. The joys.

To add insult to infection my husband went out last night to our nephew's first boxing match. I knew he would drink. He has attempted to attend two AA meetings this week. One was not there, but was replaced by a youth club being run by someone he used to work with — you can imagine his confusion. The second one he forgot his money so couldn't park. I know, I know, it all sounds rather suspect. Particularly as you can park at that time of night for free. Anyway... He told me he had one drink. I called a big lump of bullshit on that. He confessed to two. The number is irrelevant. You can't go claiming an alcohol problem and then have a drink having failed to do anything about it.

Normally around now I would say something vapid such as, 'oh well I guess it's okay for you to drink socially'. Today there is steel in my soul. I can't back down. I won't. It's been too many years of claiming to have a problem, then falling quickly into believing everything is okay. I'm not doing that any more. I'm not letting him lie to me or to himself. That is the very delusion upon which my life has been built for far too long. This time things change, and if they don't, I change them. I hate being cast as the keeper of sobriety, the one issuing threats and ultimatums. But, that's how it is.

Today is the Spring Equinox and I do feel that I stand fully between my light and my dark. This *Dirty & Divine* journey is opening my eyes to all that is true about myself. Surprising me with how I have been living... and how I thought I was living. I am being poured towards a feistier, firmer truth. I am being pulled towards the flow of an external force, a spiritual self, that only shows itself as intuition. I am being asked to shift my brain and all the influences upon it and to find something that is lasting and empowering beyond synapses and reaction.

I really want this. I need this change. I desperately want to make things work differently. There is a lot at stake. Nothing material as such. My integrity. My existence as I know it. My purity and innocence and love. I may not lose my innocence to sex, but I may well lose it to this. It makes me feel so murky, so dark, so angry. Everything is called into question and I am answering the call. I am turning up and turning out. It's a rigorous internal trip that I wasn't expecting, but that feels wholesome. Like emptying my trash, struggling to lift the bin, yet feeling so cleansed as I do away with the burdens and blocks of many moons.

Today is the fucking equinox and I am taking up a new habit of swearing more. To be a little less ladylike. A little more expansive, a little less alice and a whole lot more Alice. I can't explain it more than that. I used to think my name looked cute spelt with a little a. These days I need sharp edges and definition. I need to spring clean my name, myself, my days, my nights. I am taking a spiritual mop to my world. Confusing, perplexing, in need of deep consideration. Alice with a big fucking A.

HARNESS THE POWER OF SEVEN OF CUPS

Put all your options to the side. Consider instead what your inner feeling is. Nothing defines you other than deep down truth. Who are you without the labels, accessories, likes and dislikes?

DIRTY & DIVINE SPELLWORDS OF SEVEN OF CUPS

I look beyond the superficial and find true self.

EIGHT OF CUPS

INTUITIVE MEANING

The past is calling. And yet if you look too closely at it, you won't see what is coming in the future. Be careful to respectfully place your past behind you. Thank it for all it has brought. But now is the time to consciously move forward. Be in the moment. Right now. Rinse yourself of the dirt and grit that has clogged up your soul. Release negativity, your withheld forgiveness. Let go of 'what ifs'. Set yourself pure and clean and most importantly open to new experience and adventure.

MY JOURNEY

I have been stuck on this card for two days. Not for laziness or lack of will. But mainly because my home has been a haven of snot. It's been intense, living in the moment, mopping poorly brows, gently cleaning gunk out of eyes, those kind of things.

I rarely have the television on in the day. But to break the monotony, ring the changes and to add some colour, I had left it blaring in the background. I ventured into the living room and I was horrified to see that Brussels has been bombed.

Chaos is there. Not here. It infiltrates though, doesn't it? Where were you when 9/11 happened? Where were you when Brussels was attacked? Where were you when Pulse in Orlando or the Bataclan in Paris was shot up?

There have always been bombs. All my life. There has always been unrest of some sort. As a child I was afraid of the IRA. Growing up Iraq was the big bad fear. For a while it was Afghanistan and Bin Laden. Now it is the migrants and ISIS.

Yesterday I wanted to step off planet Earth due to the excess snot. Today I'd like to depart due to the excess violence. I've always had a problem with the violence. It makes no sense to me. None whatsoever. I'm a pacifist, a lover, a believer in life and cooperation. Yet I'm becoming numb to these big sensational killings. I hate that they fuel more violence, more war, more agenda, more propaganda. They are the reason why I rarely watch the news.

I don't know how to reconcile myself with this. The world we inhabit is shot through with a way of thinking that is not my own. So much hate. I like to think the world is raising its vibration, becoming more conscious, more loving. Yet maybe it is not. They were singing love and peace in the sixties, talking meditation, becoming flower children, protesting war, believing they were the frontier of a new loving world. What came of that? Nothing much. War and hate is a thing: a big thing. It plays out differently these days, but is the justification for so much: fear, alienation, imperialism, hate, killing, torture, rape. Why can't we all just get along, my heart cries simplistically.

It is 11:11 on 22 March and I feel like my spirit needs to depart all this. My only way to do that is to pull down the blinds and shut off the TV. I need to find my reality and live it. Love to the world. Love to the suffering. But I cannot exist in the dark. I cannot be pulled into what it spawns. So my voyage away from it is not physical, but it is mental. Focus on the good within. Live the good within. The rest, I guess, is soon to be history. Not mine though, it is not mine.

HARNESS THE POWER OF EIGHT OF CUPS

Feeling an urge to escape or travel? Create a vision board of what you would like life to look and feel like. Keep the focus on emotion and thought. Swerve away from a desire for things. How do you need to feel? Make that a focus.

DIRTY & DIVINE SPELLWORDS OF EIGHT OF CUPS

Another world lays within, I open up to let it out.

NINE OF CUPS

INTUITIVE MEANING

Dreams and wishes coming to fruition. Feeling fat full on life, smug in contentment: a pig in shit, to be blunt. But without so many negative connotations, without judgement. Allowing yourself to marinate in happiness and fulfilment without apologising for it.

MY JOURNEY

My heart is full. I've spent the last week, and more intensively the last 24 hours, caring for sick children. Not once during this time did I feel I should be someone else. My ego stepped firmly aside and my purpose was clear. Not that I should stop writing now and become a children's nurse (a more admirable vocation perhaps). But rather, there is no space for anything else when the heart takes over.

How hard it is to allow that space to open. Why it should take sickness to recognise this, I don't know. Perhaps it is this. . .

Purpose shifts. Maybe we have no singular set purpose, but many. And they overlay and undercut one another. We may grasp hold of one which makes us shine, that gives us a title and declare it our 'purpose'. Yet that stems from a patriarchal climate wherein we must know our future vocation from childhood. . . which tells us there is only one true calling, one path. What do you want to be when you grow up?

Women know that there are many worthy things to do with our time, a career being just one of them. Career and vocation are a way of fulfilling our personal potential, placating our ego, connecting to others and, if we are lucky, to an infinite source and bringing it forward through work. Yet there is much more. This is something that I feel a male-focused society has overlooked due to a fear of failure We have followed suit, making achievement the totality of our purpose. But it isn't. It isn't about that one thing. It is a hundred. A thousand.

It is having a conversation with a friend that leaves her high and flying. It is avoiding squashing that bug, or moving the spider outside instead of squishing it. It is choosing ethical ways of existing and telling our friends about them. It is those kind words you spoke to the old gent in the supermarket. It is teaching a child to ride a bike. It is reposting that wonderful Facebook meme that made you laugh. It is having a political stance. It is not having a political stance. It is reading a book. It is having a birthday party. It is singing along to your daughter's cartoons, whilst jiggling the baby and typing this badly. What are you doing right now? That is your purpose. Until it isn't. Until it shifts and a new moment of purpose overtakes it.

It is time that we, as women, helped the world to expand its purpose. Forget that. Help yourself first. You are not here to do great and wonderful things. Well, you are. But those great and wonderful things are far smaller and simpler than society would have you recognise. All that is mundane, and domestic, and gritty. That can be the very stuffing of life.

By all means seek accolades, gain certificates, grow exponentially and embrace the acclaim. I know I will, I can't help it. Yet I also know, that my purpose is not to be great, or even good, but rather to move with what comes, and to give my all to any situation.

My heart is full because for the past two days I have stood outside of all that I want, and embraced what I need to, and I did so not with resentment, but with pure love. Knowing that despite the snot and the tears and trips to the doctor, my purpose, for today, for tomorrow, is just this.

I am lucky too in that I indulge my passion. I write. I create art. I read tarot. I do what I want to do. Passion is different from purpose. If I confuse the two, then it all becomes rather vexing.

When my books become weighty with message they lose the brevity and levity of the moment. I must, in this instance, follow my passion. I am lucky that I can do that. Not everyone knows that they can, nor do they know how to.

I used to see the Nine of Cups as a card of greed. I've grown out of that. It is okay to feel fulfilled. It's okay to have passion and purpose. It's okay to know what you want. It's okay to enjoy a moment without it becoming a thing. It's okay to seek and be abundant, in whatever form that arises. It's okay to be okay.

HARNESS THE POWER OF NINE OF CUPS

Whatever brings you joy, do that.

Whomever makes your heart sing, be with them, in person, by Skype, send them an email, a prayer and a wonderful intention.

DIRTY & DIVINE SPELLWORDS OF NINE OF CUPS

I do not have a purpose: I am purpose.

TEN OF CUPS

INTUITIVE MEANING

Family, ancestry, karma and laying the past to rest. Playing out familial patterns and doing justice to them. Healing old harmful patterns visited from ancient relatives, whilst simultaneously bringing their wisdom forward. Recognising that you are a link in a chain, and that what came before, the previous links, were important, vital. They mattered. Just as you and your influence matter to your great, great, great relatives of the future.

MY JOURNEY

Last night was a full moon. It's nearly Easter. I've been asked to write a book on motherhood and one on pregnancy. Not specifically spiritual, more mindfulness and wellness. Am I qualified to write about motherhood? I'm not sure anyone is. That's not the point. We do it anyway. If it feels right, we should do it.

What an honour. To reflect and revel in the expertise of a zillion women gone past, to bring forth their knowing, to commit it to pages, read by a new generation craving a way forward, craving permission to parent how their soul wishes.

HARNESS THE POWER OF TEN CUPS

Honour your ancestors. Light a candle and send them love backwards in time, upwards in spirit. Ask for the best of them to be gifted to you. Open to their knowing.

DIRTY & DIVINE SPELLWORDS OF TEN OF CUPS

I am the gift of thousands gone before.
I honour them and accept their wisdom.

PRINCESS/PAGE OF CUPS

INTUITIVE MEANING

Life begins again. As exciting as a new start is, it can also be lonely, unreal and, at times, frightening. This card is the give and take of a new era. There is loss, potential and love all stirred together. You are not alone though. You have memories, wisdom and friends. Dig deep, little one, you are great and you have got this.

MY JOURNEY

When we are young things happen and we tend not to examine them. We take events for granted. It is only with a few more years' experience, and a little wisdom, that we can look back and see sense. The past 24 hours have been infiltrated by a woman I once knew: my first boyfriend's mother.

The fact she is arising now suggests there is some processing to do. When I was younger I cast her as the evil High Priestess, who cursed our love and pulled us apart. With age and empathy and the wanderings of my mind over this past day I'm starting to see her differently.

Archetypally she played the bad gal. A keen mix of The Empress, The High Priestess and The Hermit. For some time, I pegged her as the Evil Queen to my Snow White. I won't rehash what happened, except to say that she decided that my boyfriend and I should not be together, and she made it happen. It felt violent. It occurred overnight, literally. He had become a limb and she amputated him swiftly and without love for me. She was so instrumental in all this, that just after our split I phoned her to rake over the bones of the situation, to uncover why I had been so monumentally dumped.

She was an old fashioned Empress. To my eye at the time she was sexist, against women, but with a strong disregard for the masculine too, often destroying her husband and sons with comments aimed to fell them. She told me that I didn't do my boyfriend's washing, and, women's rights aside, she felt that I should have.

She was powerful in ways I had never previously experienced. Likeable too. Glamorous and attractive. She had run a successful business. She mothered three boys. She was spilling over with love. It poured from her with warmth and kindness... and sometimes wrath. She took me under her wing, then flung me from the nest, like a cuckoo.

What she did, effectively, is launch me into the life I have now. Her actions were the catalyst to who I have become. I have always deemed her the bad guy, but that would mean my life is now bad, coloured by her misdeeds. Yet it isn't bad. It has its grubby moments, but I am satisfied with my lot.

I guess I'm working a way towards being grateful to her. As much as I loved her son, there were many reasons we should have split, other than my lack of domesticity, and she called them all. She saw that I was too dependent. She saw we were too young. She saw we were marinating in each other and stuck in a bubble. So she threw me from the cart. I didn't go under the wheels. I flailed miserably for a while. I nearly became an air hostess. Then I made some decisions and moved onwards.

She made me the Princess of Cups, lost in a sea of love and life. She forced me to stand on my own two feet. She freed me from a love that might have turned my life a deeper shade of bland. Last night I dreamt I was furious with her. I refused to accept her decision to split me and my boyfriend apart. He didn't feature, he was just a pawn. She was the nemesis. It was a glorious mind battle that I was determined to win. She took to her bed and I went on the town with Jessa from *Girls*. I became wild and powerful. She became old and confused. I'm not sure who won. This morning, awake from the dream, I'm pretty sure it doesn't matter. It is, of course, the taking part that counts.

So I guess what I must do. . . The thing needing resolution. . . The thing about this is. . . I have something to say to her, for the pivotal role she played, the arch enemy she became. To her soul, her spirit, her feminine divine: I salute you, madam, well played. Thank you.

HARNESS THE POWER OF PRINCESS OF CUPS

Look to your hurts, to the times you have been left flailing, lonely, afraid and hurt. Find a way to see what this brought. Thank them for what they brought, who they made you.

Reach deep into the women who have affected your life. For

good, better or worse. Salute them. See what you learned. High five their divinity and aim to always wield your divinity with love, intuition and kindness.

DIRTY & DIVINE SPELLWORDS OF PRINCESS OF CUPS

From all that went before, I find my divine.

KNIGHT OF CUPS

INTUITIVE MEANING

Consider this the playboy of the pack. Resorting to stereotypes, he is the cad, the bounder, the player, the lover. He means well. He is fun and roguish. He will take your heart, but not know what do with it. He is not ready for your jelly — (thanks Beyoncé). He can be you. You can be the player too. Commitment is a big ask. And fun is fun is fun.

MY JOURNEY

We grasp quickly onto the hurts others have caused us. Our wounds are maps towards our souls. We lick them and in time they provide answers. Do we ever really contemplate the hurt we have caused others through our own uncalculated folly? It is likely you have broken someone's heart. Maybe you don't even realise it. We can have untold effects on people merely by our presence. Think upon that irritatingly gorgeous song by James Blunt. He sees a girl on the Tube. Nothing comes of it. Yet he wrote a hit sing about his love for her which catapulted money into his bank and his career into stellar mode. He didn't even speak to her. She could have been you.

Who have you hurt? Who have you dumped? Who did you enjoy for selfish fulfilment and then run from when they desired more? Oh lord. The names and events are popping into my head now. The guy who begged me not to go university so we could be together — after one evening of casual snogging. I went, of course I did. The guy who had a mega crush on me, who I kissed, because I had nothing better to do. The guy I promised I wouldn't cheat on and abandon after a holiday to Ibiza, and then I did just that. The guy who jumped off a bridge when I refused to kiss him. I refused even when I knew he would jump. He was fine, the bridge was not so high.

That's just four instances where I know someone got hurt. There are more. I won't repeat them here. My list of potential harms is too long. Most of which, to this day, I would chalk up to youthful folly. But was it to them, to the people who suffered the pain? Because I too have fallen foul of others' youthful folly, and by golly, it can hurt.

I just had to pause and hold my head in my hands as more examples spring, unwanted, to mind. The things I have done thoughtlessly, carelessly, but with, until today, very little regret.

Clearly my siren song was strong. That's not necessarily a good thing. I was enjoying myself, connecting, following my heart into a situation, then quickly backing out again. I found all these guys fascinating... until I didn't any more. I was rightfully shy of commitment and, let's be honest, I didn't really care. A guy once rang me and told me he was lonely, he was a great guy, a nice guy, a good looking and an interesting guy, I could have gone for a drink with him, but instead, I told him to get a dog.

I was mildly wild. I wasn't kind. I was once called a prick tease. Maybe more than once. I'm not concerned though with perception. I'm just 'fessing up. I've been hurt. But I've dished it out too. Nor am I apologising. Not really. That was who I was. It was fun. We all had fun. The people who got caught up in it, got emotionally invested, had their reasons, and I had mine to back off and close doors.

Life does a little dance, sometimes we are the dancer, other times the DJ. I was, for a while, the DJ. It kept me safe. I didn't get stonewalled into relationships or situations I didn't want to be in. I stopped playing when it was no longer fun. Hurting people is always going to be a side effect of life, a side effect of fun.

I hold my hands up. Guilty, your honour. I'm a reformed character now. My fun is no longer sought through dalliances with dudes, but in other ways. That is growing up for you. One day the Knight of Cups will grow up too. He will find love, settle down, have kids maybe. His kids will rinse and repeat and through this lessons will arise, babies will be born, emotions will be tattered and hearts slain then rejigged. The human race continues in awe and antipathy, getting by and getting high. One daft move after the next.

HARNESS THE POWER OF KNIGHT OF CUPS

Dwell not on where it hurt, but instead focus on the fun that was had. Emotional pain comes when the fun ends, when the love ends. Make a choice to be thankful for the good stuff that was brought. Take heart from the fact that the end of the fun was not an error, but as inevitable and as essential as breath.

DIRTY *&* DIVINE SPELLWORDS OF KNIGHT OF CUPS

I will find fun; I am the fun.

QUEEN OF CUPS

INTUITIVE MEANING

Emotional depth. The rivers of feeling expanding within to create all that is to be felt within human flesh. The mother of all. The lover of all. The wife of the world. Loved. Mistreated. Adored. Revered. Oblivious to it all. In a state of meditation and harmony with all that she loves. At one with the world, intuitive, heartfelt and knowing.

MY JOURNEY

I am fuzzy with devotion. I have spent the best part of a month caring for my sick children. My daily jaunts have been whittled down to trips to the doctors, and yesterday, to the hospital. I know my way round our local hospital thanks to an ongoing review of my baby's potential kidney situation. Yesterday a gurney went past me. Zipped up and covered over, two sombre nurses pushing it. Death so very close and yet so far removed.

I hate to become morose. That's not the point of this. Yet it is being deeply dark with death that we are spun back towards love and life. Surrounded by sick people in a hospital, each dancing with disease and misfortune, I can't help but count my blessings.

Life is short and emotions are long. My emotions, since becoming a mother, are intricately tied to the shortness of life. People lose people and women lose children, every day. Having created life, I see the fine line between nurturing it, and it being swept away. That thought could send me into madness.

Sometimes I glimpse myself unconsciously on a soul level whispering: I don't want to be in this life any more. It is such a quiet plea. It could go past unnoticed. I am far from suicidal. Rather it is an admission from deep within that the love I hold, so brave, so empowering, so colourful, is in fact rather fragile. It wants to go home.

There is only one antidote to that. It is to sweep those I love into my arms and to give of myself. I swallow down the lump of fear and I hold what I have. I kiss foreheads and pretend that this will last forever. And it will. But not quite like this. Not always in the crook of my arm or tangled around my body in bed, snotty snores in my ear and little fingers deftly threaded through my hair.

HARNESS THE POWER OF QUEEN OF CUPS

What fears does your love provoke? Take any fear of loss and transmute it into passion for the moment. Grab your partner, kids, dog or friends and be in the moment.

DIRTY *&* DIVINE SPELLWORDS OF QUEEN OF CUPS

Love is forever. I am forever. I am love.

KING OF CUPS

INTUITIVE MEANING

A masculine maturity of emotion. The ability to balance feelings. This could represent a husband, partner, beloved male friend or loving father figure. He represents unconditional love, strength and possibility. He has a heart full of emotions and offers great healing. He is a good guy. A family guy. A guy who puts others first and has a bucket load of self-awareness that renders him wise, warm and witty.

MY JOURNEY

Today started off in a lovely way. My husband had designed an Easter treasure hunt for our eldest. It was fabulous.

The day took a swerve to the miserable though soon after the hunt. As well as being Easter, it is also my mother-in-law's birthday. I had decided not to go, as I and the baby are both unwell. Having nursed both girls through weeks of poorliness, it was a great opportunity to have a rest whilst my husband took the eldest.

He has, in recent days, been pretty good. He is clearly suffering with anxiety though and gets overwhelmed easily. The thought of attending this family event, sober and without me, seemed to be daunting him. He had his strained face on and was generally snappy and full of worry.

I don't get it. I try to. But I'm not an anxious person. As a teenager I had a period of self-consciousness, but it passed. I'm lucky. I feel that my husband is lucky, he has a family who all live in the same town and who get to meet for birthdays and Christmas and for no reason whatsoever. I don't have that. Growing up parts of my family were on the other side of the country and the other side of the Atlantic. I kinda wish I had them closer.

With a little foresight I know he will come back having had a lovely time, having left all the anxiety behind him. Yet I'm not the one feeling the panic and the overwhelm: he is. He can get up on a stage and perform in front of thousands, sober might I add (he never drinks before gigs). He can be the cockiest, swaggeriest dude in the room, when it suits him. Yet place him in the periphery of a family event, or a meeting with good friends, and he loses all ability to cope. He is miserable in the lead up to it. Though he always comes home having had a fabulous time.

So he was vexed this morning. He walks into a room, and without saying anything I feel it. I feel it all over the place. It feels like anger, frustration and just plain vehemence. It's there in his persona, his aura, his breath. I really want to make it go away. I reel out all the one liners, 'it'll be okay', 'you will have fun', 'what's the worst that can happen?'. I'm oblivious to how to make it cease. And I hate it.

This is, of course, more about me, because it is my journey. I would wish for emotional maturity for him, but, perhaps I ought to pray for a dose for me too. I pray I wouldn't react. I pray I could just ignore it. I pray I could say the right thing. I pray that when they come home again later, all will be well, fun will have been had, and the mood will have evaporated.

Anxiety is shit. It brings naught but drama to the door. It's a real thing though. It's a truly real thing. It causes so much pain. My spiritual proclamations do nothing to make it stop. It is catching too, because I get anxious about anxiety, then all hell breaks loose.

I'm happy to report that we did better today. What normally is a battle of he said, she said, became something deeper. Under the powerful hand of The King of Cups we sat and talked. We got deep. Whilst I no further understand why my husband feels as he does, I do better understand what he is feeling.

HARNESS THE POWER OF KING OF CUPS

Think on strong and loving males and/or masculine figures in your life (real life, or characters and icons you admire). Who are they? What do they bring?

Consider the male aspects of yourself. Have you ever felt 'manly' or aligned to a masculine part of yourself? When was that and how did it feel? Send love to this part, ask it to bring forward its guidance.

Think on Daddy issues. . . Is, or was, your father (or father figure) present and loving? If not, what did he gift to you, even if only an inner strength to survive him? View the relationship (or lack thereof) with your father as a gift. Seek the good.

DIRTY & DIVINE SPELLWORDS OF KING OF CUPS

I open my heart to loving masculine power.

THE PENTACLES

I don't feel comfortable with the Pentacles (also known as Coins), which is why I have chosen them next. But rather than sitting back passively and allowing them to lead, I'm trying something else. I have decided to get outside of my comfort zone. The Coins are just that, cards representing money, materialism, abundance and, of course, lack thereof. I will embrace all things abundant. I expect big things. I place an intention to receive and I am letting the Pentacles work for me, rather than working around me.

I believe that is the way abundance works. You place something into the world, and you think big positive thoughts. Moreover, you do this for the right reason. I feel like, finally, I am cracking onto the right reason. I want an abundant life: not for acclaim, not for a bigger house, not for fortune, but rather to enable me to live the life I want to feel. I want to feel healthy, contented, and I want to be with my kids, without the pressure of a day job. I want to receive my abundance, doing what I do, doing what I love and at the same time, being with those I love.

I have bridges to cross. I was brought up with somewhat of a poverty mentality. I always felt like the poorest kid in the well-off village that we lived in. I had 'dinner tickets' instead of money. We got our school uniform from some place where you didn't have to pay, but the choice was weak, acrylic and cheap. On a worldwide scale, we did okay. There was always food in the cupboards. There were treats. We lived in an abundantly beautiful place. But I was drilled with fear concerning cold hard cash. There was not enough, it seemed.

I started working from a young age: babysitting, waitressing, working in the local pub. I loved it. Oh, how I wish I could love working in a pub now as I did then: such a simple, fun, booze-filled life! I went to university and was the lucky recipient of grants and loans — back when that kind of thing was available. I got decent jobs as a result. I was, however, unfocused. The jobs I did only semi-fit into my life plan. They were people-focused. They made some small difference. Yet they didn't fulfil my soul; how I wished they would.

It turned out what I really wanted to do was write. Ah. That. The thing I had seen two different parental figures struggling to do in any kind of way that provided payment. I started off with that curse to overcome. Five books down the line and I am actively trying to overcome that. That is the thing I want to hop, skip and jump over. It is a hurdle I am getting ready to jump. I receive pennies for my words, thus far. I am getting ready to receive pounds. I am placing my energy out, and expecting energy back. The energy of money.

There is one thing I do know though. When it becomes about the money, it stops being fun. That has been my experience. Though that is when I deflect from writing and try some offshoot venture. That tends to leave me tired and wanting.

So, what about if I plough all my energy into my one true love? What about that? What if I believe that it can bring what I desire and need? Writers can and do make money and attract abundance. I can provide for the life I desire. I am here to do just that. I never really have, because I never really felt it possible. I can give and receive, all by doing only what I feel is my vocational purpose. These positive affirmations are my beacon to the universe. Let's test them.

So I begin the journey of The Pentacles with all that in mind. I am not letting it happen to me any more. Instead, I am playing my part, stepping up, throwing myself out into whatever kindness and fortune favours me.

ACE OF PENTACLES

INTUITIVE MEANING

A new material start, a fresh financial approach. The birth of new material abundance. An idea gifted, as if from the heavens. Inspiration in terms of work, career and business. The purpose of soul, meddling with the purpose of life and finding a way forward that involves both.

MY JOURNEY

I put some feelers out about my books with publishers and friends who have the inside track. I'd been putting this off for weeks, holding back. It is never time until you make the time. I made it.

I also tidied up some writing and proposals in the full belief they are my purpose and will get the attention necessary: I will send them out soon.

And then I close down my laptop and go for an Indian meal with my family. This thing is about balance. I can attract what I need, and what I need most right now is my family and providing for them. So I must do that. Act it, be it, bring it.

HARNESS THE POWER OF ACE OF PENTACLES

What are you holding back on creating? Do it now. Get started. Evolve projects. Share yourself.

Plan why you want to attract money, abundance or comfort. Not for its own sake. But rather think about how you would like to feel, who you need to support and what you want to bring, truly. Make your abundance mean something. Not a car, not a holiday home, but something tangible that improves lives and provides for the lifestyle that counts.

Live as if you are successful in your manifestation. Enjoy your day. Trust that what you need is coming and all you need do is dance the necessary steps as you move towards it.

Follow your passion. Cut loose dead ends. Release ties to things that pay, but don't fulfil. This doesn't have to be literal. You may not wish to up and quit your job. But you can psychically release your dependence upon it. Whilst simultaneously moving towards what you want to be doing, emotionally, mentally, literally.

DIRTY & DIVINE SPELLWORDS OF ACE OF PENTACLES

With love and faith, I create what I desire.

TWO OF PENTACLES

INTUITIVE MEANING

Getting your priorities in order. Paying attention to detail and creating balance. The options laid ahead of you may not be so different from one another. This in itself causes confusion and friction. Yet these are just feelings. Those decisions that lay ahead are identikit versions of life. Either way, you are likely to get where you don't know you are going anyway.

MY JOURNEY

It is the first day after a Bank Holiday weekend when the clocks went forward and I am a bit bored and flummoxed.

Sometimes to get back on track you have to sludge through all kinds of puddles of moodiness. I'd love to blame my period for this one. It is a very PMS-feeling day. Yet I'm breastfeeding and I'm not having periods, so my hormones can't even take the blame. I'm not in sync with anything lunar or biological: I'm just plain unbalanced.

So I will plough through today. Tomorrow we have plans, and by golly do we need them. I need to get back to the positivity and power I espoused only yesterday when writing of my grand plans to make the Coins work for me. Right now the only way coins have worked for me was spilling out of my handbag, all over the floor, just when I needed to be leaving the house. Which is great, money is spilling in my direction. Just not quite in the way I'd desired! Funny, universe, funny! Oh, and there were the three tax demand letters that arrived today too, let's not forget that. . .

I will power through this sludge, in whole faith that I must knock these blocks to get where I want to be.

HARNESS THE POWER OF TWO OF PENTACLES

Balance your books. Financially or otherwise. If things are off-kilter, examine why and pour energy where it is needed. Collect your pennies, pay your bills (or arrange a repayment plan). Get things straight.

DIRTY *&* DIVINE SPELLWORDS OF TWO OF PENTACLES

I create balance to enable abundance.

THREE OF PENTACLES

INTUITIVE MEANING

Success or growth of a project. Things working out well. Teaming up with others to grow and to collaborate. Efforts placed, with dignity and devotion, towards growth. Attention to detail, whilst patiently and slowly building a bigger picture.

MY JOURNEY

I'm in a better mood today. Balance is restored and I had a lovely day with a good friend and her son. It was just what we all needed to wash away a fortnight of being under the weather, literally as well as health wise.

I was wondering about my commitment to the Coins, to making a step career-wise, when I received a very tempting offer. I am not one to advertise my wares. My primary concern is my writing, but I do also undertake private tarot readings for an array of international clients. I am serious about expanding that service. The email offer provided for that, at a very reasonable rate, and with a money back guarantee should I not be happy. Such unusual and ethical advertising I rarely see. So I went for it. I signed up to advertise my readings. Something I have thus far avoided as word of mouth has been sufficient. Whether this proves to be a test of my tarot metal or a red herring remains to be seen.

HARNESS THE POWER OF THREE OF PENTACLES

Educate, collaborate and contribute. See your desires as ever-evolving and allow new knowledge to influence you. Nothing is static. Grow with your plans.

DIRTY & DIVINE SPELLWORDS OF THREE OF PENTACLES

I allow my ambition to carry me to places I had not envisaged.

FOUR OF PENTACLES

INTUITIVE MEANING

Be careful with what you have. Allocate funds wisely. Keep a little for the heart, a little for the soul, a little for the overheads and a little stashed away for uncertainties. Money may feel like a prison. But within those jailhouse walls you can hatch an escape plan.

MY JOURNEY

Today I recognised that the Pentacles don't just make things change. I must put the work in to enable change to come forward. For a while now I have been making small alterations to my website and wondering why nothing there was really working. I get a good hit of visitors, but no rewards. So I took the question to a business women's group I am a member of. I felt rather amateur posing the question, but they didn't patronise. They gave me answers. I have heeded their advice and re-built my website from scratch almost.

I had always held my website to be more an informational one than a shop. Then I wondered why I didn't sell anything. The site is now turned around on itself, and the whole thing is built around the shop. That feels so unnatural, yet, that's what I need to do. I need to go against my own grain, get uncomfortable, admit to myself and the paying world that I have things to offer, things worthy of a price, things that need not be hidden modestly beneath an overly complex front.

If I am to attract abundance I need not feel ashamed of it. I must open the channels in all ways that I can. I must plough through the feeling that I can't or shouldn't make money. Do you know that feeling? I'm not sure it stems entirely from family. I think in part it is a 'woman thing'. For centuries we were not the providers, not the money makers, such a thought was obscene and against nature. So of course it feels wrong and sordid to try to make some cash, to attempt to pay the mortgage. There is a cultural ghost of that within our very DNA. It's a ghost that I need to lay to rest. I will not be haunted. I will expand, I will grow. I will become at one with the energy of finance.

I've never had a problem receiving money from a finite source such as a wage. It is the idea of making my own money that has always stuck. I was raised to follow a particular life path. A safe path whereby a third party paid me, allowed me holiday, sick pay and ensured I worked within their supportive and structured framework. That was the pinnacle of what I was asked to achieve. And it is a very sensible ask, very reasonable indeed.

Making money, all on my own, without an institution being in charge: now that is just new and weird and terrifying. Yet I am doing it. Thus far it's been pocket change. Yet there are millions of people and billions of units of cash to go around. I'm just asking for a me-sized chunk. Enough to do what I want with.

So I have structured my website, my public presence, around making money. Not just my tarot, but my books too. I have stuff to sell. I am worthy of that exchange. I can take as well as give. This will be interesting.

HARNESS THE POWER OF FOUR OF PENTACLES

Consider any fears about your relationship with money. In particular, breaking from any expectations placed upon you by culture, parents and ancestral lines, in relation to earning. What is it about receiving that scares you? Meditate on that with an aim of moving past it.

Open your channels to receive. In whatever way works for you. Don't sit tight on what you have. Open gloriously to more, even if that is simply setting an intention.

DIRTY & DIVINE SPELLWORDS OF FOUR OF PENTACLES

I receive what I deserve. I am deserving of all I hope for.

FIVE OF PENTACLES

INTUITIVE MEANING

The card depicts a mindset (and a current reality) of poverty, envy and fear. We will always stay small if we are blinded to our blessings and lusting after the varied wealth of others. Our path is as perfect as it can be for the moment. It is perfect for who we will later become. Blind yourself to the success and failures of others and pour the energy of that envy into the world you, and you alone, are creating for yourself.

MY JOURNEY

I'm excited. Remember I mentioned to you about being asked to write two books, and getting paid to do it? Well, that is looking likely to go ahead. Whereas all my other projects flounder uselessly, even with a change of website and the advertising I undertook. What does this say to me? It tells me this simple truth: what is meant to move, will do so. That which is not for us, or not quite for us, will not flow. It may stop, and start and occasionally look like a good thing. Then it will stall, leaving you stranded and questioning.

When you follow, wholeheartedly, that which you love the most, there is every chance it will succeed. I believe we are gifted our loves for a reason. There is a reason some people love science and others love animals and some love mathematics. There is a reason I love to write. Whilst there a thousands of other careers I could push halfway, writing is the only one for me that seems to flow, that I adore, and that is my passion.

When I divert from that passion I get caught up in making money. Whereas making money from writing is like a gift on top of a gift. I love writing enough to not need to make money from it. I love it enough for it to be a forever hobby. The fact I have set out to earn money from my writing, and the fact it is happening, tells me so much about purpose, the law of attraction and that some things are just meant to be.

I could continue to think small, to keep my writing tight and close. Yet this feels like the universe's permission to take what is mine and to be cool with it. To humbly and proudly and excitedly step into a new vein of life. One where I get paid to do what I love. Over and over again. Moreover, to write about what I love. To write for you. To write in ways that change lives for the better, my own very much included.

It has taken years for this to come to any kind of fruition. The block to this blossoming was always me. I never believed. I never really tried to believe. I made the wish to the universe, then got distracted. Since having children my resolve has strengthened. My need to make money, to grow and expand has new underlying reason. I'm not doing it for fame, fortune or acclaim. I'm doing it for my family. So I get to do what I love, and the plan is that it will provide for me to be with the people I love. This could, perhaps, be a slice of heaven. A hardworking, gritty kind of heaven, one with nappies and tantrums and sneaking off into dark rooms to plough out a paragraph whilst Daddy and daughter giggle next door. A very human, woman-made heaven. And I'm making it, I'm really making it.

Let me be honest. After writing the above I felt a very real shudder of doubt and fear. Who am I to get paid to write about anything? I haven't studied writing. I have no qualifications or certificates or acclaim in the subjects of motherhood or pregnancy. I'm a fake. I'm a fraud. I'm going to get found out.

I let the shudder pass and I reminded myself that there is no truth to it. I may write. I may do whatever I please. I may be successful, I may not. None of that matters. What counts is following my passion to wherever it takes me.

As I wrote this, my daughter brought my iPad into me. She is watching a few nursery rhymes. 'Look, Mummy,' she said, 'you used to sing this to me.' I listened closer to the lady dressed as a dancing bear. And there it was, one of my favourite hymns from childhood. Perfectly appropriate truth. . . 'This little light of mine, I'm gonna let it shine, let it shine, let it shine!'

HARNESS THE POWER OF FIVE OF PENTACLES

Look to your path and count your blessings. Drop the comparisons that make you feel bad about your lot. Focus instead on what you do have. Make the most of it just for today. Find joy in the present and know that you are where you need to be, for now.

DIRTY & DIVINE SPELLWORDS OF FIVE OF PENTACLES

I find joy in my path.

SIX OF PENTACLES

INTUITIVE MEANING

Giving generously, receiving gratefully. Creating and seeking peace with what you have. Knowing that the secret to abundance is sharing. Being aware and conscious with your cash and your prosperity. Charity, being the giver, and at times the appreciative recipient.

MY JOURNEY

I'm stretching my finances right now. I am on the poor end of my maternity leave and so I am carefully spending, whilst also working to attract more. I am exploring a happy attitude to cash right now. In the lead up to this period of time money has quite nicely balanced itself. Mortgage payments have gone down, allowing for a new car payment to fill that gap. The outgoings remain roughly the same in spite of new necessities (boiler repair, washing machine, two new car tyres, broken toilet, amongst many other domestic catastrophes) pulling on our wages.

Rather than curse the requirements to spend out on unexpected bills, I'm taking it in my stride. I'm expecting more. I won't give into fear of lack. I know it will be just fine. The cosmos is going to provide and so I act rationally and with care to conserving the small amount we do have and utilising it wisely.

We spent the day socialising, at home. Cheap and cheerful. We kept the cost low and gave as we could. A bottle of wine for the grown-ups and homemade cookies for the kids. Friendship need not cost a great deal, and we were gifted with gorgeous weather, which costs nothing and gives so much.

HARNESS THE POWER OF SIX OF PENTACLES

Give of yourself. Give your time, your smile, your love, your money, your wisdom. Whatever suits. Trust that in the scheme of life it doesn't matter if you are on the giving or receiving end, done well and with love, they both feel the same.

DIRTY & DIVINE SPELLWORDS OF SIX OF PENTACLES

I expect to give; I expect to take.

SEVEN OF PENTACLES

INTUITIVE MEANING

Appreciating the benefits of your successes thus far. Stepping back and recognising the distance gained. You have come far, be a little in awe of all you can reap from your experiences and efforts.

MY JOURNEY

Today was a day of great contrast. It started with so much fun. The girls and I played together, wrestling on the bed. My husband came in and looked at me agog and simply said, 'How are you so happy?' The answer: I'm not wholly sure. I just enjoy the moment. I let little things slip by without investing much emotional stress.

I'm by no means perfect. Halfway through the day my baby had a coughing fit that bordered on choking. I called emergency services, and, of course, by the time they answered she was fine. It all led to me taking her to the hospital for a check over. Though a Sunday spent at the hospital and then stuck in a traffic jam caused by the football letting out, was not my plan. I sat in that car, barely moving, as fans in droves passed me by. The baby was exhausted and whilst distracted for a little by toys, soon became hysterical. I sang to her, I stroked her face and horribly she sobbed herself to sleep whilst we crept slowly through the town.

I felt pretty damned sorry for myself after this. I found myself sliding into a little funk. I caught myself planning how I would play upon this dire set of events when I got home. I heard my mind concocting a little pity party, whereby I would receive much tea and sympathy from the husband. But then I stopped in my tracks and counted my blessings: 1) the baby is fine 2) she is mercifully and finally asleep and no longer crying 3) the baby is fine. So I dug deep into the Taylor Swift refrain to, 'shake it off' and that is what I did. By the time I got home my good mood was restored.

I could have chosen to play on the feeling of frustration I had. I could have bemoaned the events to my husband, hoping for some empathy. I very nearly did. But what would it have brought me? Tea and sympathy? I got that anyway without creating more drama, without evoking feelings that I didn't necessarily need to be feeling. Most often our emotions are a choice. It is easy to get pulled under by them and truly believe that this is where we should belong. It is just as easy to shake them off. So I guess this is the response to my husband as to why I am so happy. I refuse to dwell. I jump out of foggy moods. I don't wholeheartedly become my mood, I acknowledge it and let it pass. I look to the good and that usually dispels the bad pretty quickly.

HARNESS THE POWER OF SEVEN OF PENTACLES

Whatever situation dogs you, actively aim to shake it off. Catch yourself falling into pity and raise yourself up and out of it.

DIRTY *&* DIVINE SPELLWORDS OF
SEVEN OF PENTACLES

My feeling is a choice. I raise my feeling high.

EIGHT OF PENTACLES

INTUITIVE MEANING

This card reflects the learning of a trade. Becoming at one with the role in life we want to undertake, learning through passion, work and perseverance. The true grit of work that lays behind future success.

MY JOURNEY

I felt a slow flood of worry arise around me today. I have so many blessings of abundance very nearly in the bag, and yet nothing is certain, nor is it enough. I am so consumed with my writing that I forget I have a day job to return to. The day job is currently paying my maternity leave. Soon I will be on leave, but without any payment. I am focusing on long term goals, and wonderful opportunities appear to be on the horizon. But what about next month's mortgage?

I stopped that line of thinking. It was quickly slipping towards the negativity I have been studiously avoiding as I travel through the Pentacles. It is early April, it's sunny but cold. I went outside with my three-year-old daughter for some fresh air. She took it upon herself to turn the hose on and soak me. I resisted at first, paranoid about colds and germs, adult reservations holding firm. Then I thought, sod it, and we both ended up freezing cold and drenched. As I type, a pile of our clothes sit sodden by the back door.

This figurative downpour cleared my brain. It made space for a realisation. I am being offered precisely what I asked for. I requested the universe provide for my extended maternity leave. That was my intention a few months back. All I wanted, all I cared about, was covering that period of time. I didn't ask for more: it felt humbler to simply ask for what I needed, the bare bones. Enough for that mortgage situation. And it very much looks like my luck is in, that period, those bare bones, are about to be covered.

I have received what I wanted. So why do I feel robbed, as though I do not have enough, as if I need something more? What has happened though, is that as the money for maternity leave has come to me, I've started adding to that initial desire. I want a holiday. At the least. But that wasn't what I asked for. It wasn't what I prayed for. I've got greedy. I've got ungrateful. Instead of seeing how I'm being provided for I've upped the ante and feel offended and frustrated that I haven't got my new tick list fulfilled. Yet my original one has been. It truly has. I see that now.

It's so easy to get what we wanted and not see it clearly. This has taught me something important: don't be modest if you can't deal with the outcome. Go bigger if you must. I attracted exactly what I asked for. So I can do it again. Maybe next time I will stretch further with my desires, just to cover a holiday of course.

It's not the end. I have learned a valuable lesson. You get what you ask for, so be careful in expressing those desires. I desperately wanted to be with my baby a whole year. That has been granted. That was my big desire. It's done. I should be singing from the rooftops. I will.

Excitingly I see now that with the right feeling, the correct intent, and a good reason I can attract all I hope for. I can forever be open to some kind of abundance. I shared this with my husband and his initial reaction was that his wishes have never come true, that he had been looking for musical success since he was a kid, that the law didn't apply to him because his dreams didn't happen. I pointed out to him the following. What he had done with music was impressive and that if he were to tell his kid self about it, said kid would be deeply impressed. I also pointed out that the desires of his kid self may not be relevant any more. He has been there, done that and he has moved past it.

Maybe it is time to tweak and modify his intent, twist it round to better suit his current existence. He did get what he wished for as a fourteen-year-old youth hooked on MTV, and it wasn't what he needed, but he got it. He made it happen. To a very real extent. Yes, he could have gone further. But the person who actually blocked that happening was him. Sometimes we create our own downfalls. Sometimes we ask for something then freak the fuck out when it arises. Sometimes what we wanted is actually horrible for us. When that happens it is time to make new wishes.

I see dreams coming true all the time. My daughter is forever making her desires known. And invariably they come true. She says something, five minutes later, it happens. She is forever saying, 'ah my wish came true again, Mummy'. I'm in awe, because sometimes what she wishes for are things I actively try to prevent, and yet somehow the universe conspires to her whim and I stand by helpless and impressed. She makes shit happen day in and day out, just by expressing a belief that it should and she would rather like it to. She hasn't got any adult doubt, about herself, or about her ability to bring something to her. So it just happens. The purity, the simple passion behind her wish, it all adds up to success time and time again.

Knowing I too can do that, that I can access the infinite and pull it round to my advantage and that I do deserve it, is a powerful set of thoughts. So I will be grateful for the desires I have had granted. I won't add to the shopping list after it's been checked out. I'll simply write a new one. What a fascinating lesson. I got exactly what I asked for.

HARNESS THE POWER OF EIGHT OF PENTACLES

What are you a student of today? Adulthood, certification, education do not necessarily add up to expertise. What more can you learn? What of your life requires further knowledge? Syphon the segments of need and commit to becoming a pupil, open yourself to not knowing it all, and move gratefully toward knowledge.

DIRTY & DIVINE SPELLWORDS OF EIGHT OF PENTACLES

I embrace all that I have yet to learn.

NINE OF PENTACLES

INTUITIVE MEANING

Take some time to enjoy what you have created. This card asks you to step away from work, take a break, enjoy the flowers, nature and just being. You deserve it. And from this place you will gain perspective, learning and new creative energy to refresh your soul. Actively place some of your money towards a fun venture. Take a day off. Take a holiday. Pay for a treat for yourself and feel the energetic flow of your work rewarding you, not just in terms of money, but in terms of what that money can provide for you.

MY JOURNEY

Alongside yesterday's blossoming understanding that I can attract all I like, I felt wholly empowered today. I visited a wonderful friend living in a luxurious and spacious new home, I spent time with family and indulged in their abundant being. In the evening we had blissful family time.

Life feels abundant today. Whilst I strive for monetary success, the cards continue to remind me that it is not particularly important. I have learned that I can create at the least what I need, and so my next aim is to manifest more of the same, more comfort, more belonging, more money energy with which to enable the relative luxury in which I live.

It is relevant luxury. I'm not holed up in a mansion. I'm residing in a three-bed semi in a large village in the middle of England. It's by no means a palace. But it's more than many, many people on this planet have. It's easy to forget that and to lust for more. And I do lust. That is a pathological part of our society. My ultimate goal would be an old farmhouse and a big garden with room for a goat, some chickens and a vegetable patch. I might never leave that plot again should I ever land in it. Yet what I have already is more than enough. Even my poverty-stricken youth was played out in relevant luxury. We have so much, we don't see it. We are snow-blind to our abundance.

So I aim to be grateful for it, and yet not ashamed of the gentle lust for more. That is a human trait. What matters though is not usurping our desire with guilt, but rather, taming that desire with appreciation. I appreciate what I have here. I've done good. It's nice, it's ours, it's far superior to the shacks I witnessed in the Dominican Republic, it is a world away from the tents housing migrants just over the little ocean in Calais, it is spectacularly grand compared to the doorway I saw two people living in the other day.

We all deserve more. Especially those with less. So for now I praise and invoke a wish for more, tempered with full appreciation of all that I already have, and a continued hope for a fairer world whereby all might share in the simple, easy luxury of something akin to middle England.

HARNESS THE POWER OF NINE OF PENTACLES

Take some time out of your ambitions. Put your drive to the side. Instead luxuriate in what you have and allow feelings of appreciation to expand.

DIRTY & DIVINE SPELLWORDS OF
NINE OF PENTACLES

I have so much already.

TEN OF PENTACLES

INTUITIVE MEANING

Family issues are arising. Perhaps relating to your immediate family, but also ancestral, karmic issues. All of us are born, laden down with the hopes wishes, fears and foibles of previous generations. Sometimes we are birthed to help correct and amend hundreds of years of issues that have been passed down. In doing this we heal our lives and this echoes back through time to our ancestors and to their spirit. Heal the past and set it free. Create a clean slate for future generations. At the same time, own what is worthy from your lineage. Accept the wisdom that powers down the genetic line. Take it and wield it with pride.

MY JOURNEY

My mum had been in the US for several weeks and a lunch has been arranged to get us all back together. In recent years my mum, dad and stepmums (yes, I have two, one partnered to

Mum, the other to Dad) have all been, not only on talking terms, but socializing terms, so my dad and stepmum were in attendance too. It was a lovely day. My mum's civil partner was not there, but in her wake she had left a delicious meal. My brother and his wife came along, which is still a novelty as it was only fairly recently that they moved to the UK from Tokyo.

It's a lovely thing to have (nearly) everyone all in one room, especially as a child of divorce. My mum commented on how they all had moved on from the past. Without mentioning the specifics and weird animosities of my childhood, it is apparent that age, time and wisdom has played its part and there is the seed of friendliness between my parents. These social events are happening more often, and as Mum lives in the middle of many of us, she is the instigator. I guess marriages, adult children and grandchildren have a way of providing for a new cohesion.

I'm not even sorry that this didn't happen many years ago. Divorce has its well-recognised shit. People are burned by it. Situations are made unwieldy and venomous. People are influenced by their hurt, by the cultural expectations, by new partners, by the unrelenting task of still raising the children of that marriage in some semblance of normality. As I have the belief that all things happen for a reason, I find it all quite charming. The divorce shaped me into who I am, and at least, some decades later, there is a resolve, a peace, a white flag over the crumbs of a love that, if nothing else, spurned three rather awesome kids and then later, three (so far) rather awesome grandkids.

As an adult it's easy to feel above and beyond one's parents. To feel as though you have somehow taken their mantle and improved upon it, perhaps even flown far from it. Yet here, in this place, I see how I began. I see aspects of myself popping up around the dinner table in a mannerism, in an interest, in a way of seeing the world. To feel the support of those parents, continuing into adulthood is a gorgeous thing too. Having my writerly and spiritual father say that this book, which he is currently reading, is the best I have ever written, still makes me feel like I just did so well on my school report. To see my mum's joy at the baby eating (as opposed to the first baby who didn't eat much) still makes me feel proud of myself, in ways that I resisted with the first.

After many moons of doing it for myself, of living in my bubble, I see I am returned to youth, that little girl who lived under the gaze of her parents, so quickly. One thing happened today that really amused me and captured my attention. At one point I asked my dad a question about a book he was reading. He was answering and somehow I got distracted by my little brother, like a typical kid I tuned out and engaged with my bro instead. Suddenly my mum piped up,

'Alice, listen to your father.'

It has been some thirty years since she last said that to me. And you know what, I did. I obeyed, automatically, without a second thought. I took the verbal rap on the wrist and heard Daddy out. Full circle was achieved and all that I came from rose up to meet me.

There is no escape, people. We are the beauty and the trauma and wonder of our ancestors, our parents, our tribes. From here we always begin. Today I was the Princess, free in her own right, having achieved my own adulthood, my own successes. I have followed my path, my desires, just like the Princess of Coins. I am materially sound; I am mentally safe. I am my own woman. But I am somebody's baby too. There is a spiral here somewhere. One where I can be all things: a mother, a child, a princess, a queen. It shifts and I shift.

HARNESS THE POWER OF TEN OF PENTACLES

Think on your parents, grandparents and siblings. What have they brought you? Look at who they have shaped you into. These people, laden with them as we are, carry great gifts, amazing learning. Sometimes that plays out through drama, other times through comradeship. Often a little of both. Who are these souls that have shaped you, and what have they brought to your current path?

DIRTY *&* DIVINE SPELLWORDS OF
TEN OF PENTACLES

You, (. . .), were sent to help me understand myself.

PRINCESS/PAGE OF PENTACLES

INTUITIVE MEANING

The innocence and excitement of a new materially abundant idea. Harnessing that excitement, ploughing through doubt and making initial plans, schemes and visualisations. The dreaming and creative beginning of something you don't quite feel ready for, but that calls all the same. This Princess is ready to grow. She has the excitement of a child, and the wiles of a teenager. She may wish to create and harvest something the world is not quite ready for. Perhaps she has been discouraged in the past. Yet her soul is ready for venture and adventure. She is ready to grow from her loins, from her womb, from the abilities, that she, if nobody else, has total faith in.

MY JOURNEY

A scheme came together and my maternity leave is now fully sorted, stable and most importantly doable. As I began to consider scrabbling around for a plan B, the cosmos came through. Thank goodness, I was not ready to leave my hatchlings in their nest quite yet.

The moment this happened I literally felt the weight fall from me. Already my desire for that 'little bit more' from my new financial shopping list is starting to pay off. More is coming. Not yet my millions. Still it is just enough, and indeed will also pay for that longed for holiday. It's been a quick turnaround.

I didn't used to believe in the ability to manifest or attract. I thought it was perhaps a little distasteful and unspiritual. The world can be a hard and cold place, to ask for comfort and support somehow seemed a little 'off'. Indeed, many of my attempts to manifest failed flat, especially when it came to money. Yet the self-help genre is filled with books, CDs and meditations that promise great riches, success and power should we just place our minds in the right direction and keep our intent pure.

Manifestation, for all intents and purposes, has become a skewed and holified version of capitalism. If we are aiming to manifest stuff, for stuff's sake, we are utterly missing the point. Yes, you might pull forth that longed for car, purse or cash injection. But I believe the manifestation will stop flat there if you don't make the connection. The connection being that you are connected to all things and life can be miraculous if you choose to open your eyes to it. If instead you continue to utilise the law of attraction to bring you more shit, the law of attraction will place you to the back of the queue. Your divine self will step up and say, 'she doesn't get it'. Your divine self will call some serious bullshit on you.

Manifestation is a very real thing. But if you don't give back, if you don't build it into a much bigger sacred picture, then it ceases to exist for you. The key is not in making the wish in the right way (there is no right way), it is in living the wish, and being open to that wish provoking a new life. Indeed, are you attending to the wishes of others? Albeit perhaps unconsciously. Are you doing the most you can with your world? Are you living to the highest degree? Are you offering yourself to others in kindness, in love, in truth? And until you do that, and trust me, I'm not wholly doing it either, then why should you manifest anything? Manifestation is a spiritual job, a career even. You have to give to get. You have to seek to find. You don't just make a vision board and get back to being a loathsome buffoon. That shit won't wash. You want it? You live it.

Once you get to a certain degree of spiritual living, the place whereby manifestation becomes easier, it is very likely that what you wanted at the start of your trip, will have significantly changed anyway. That, of course, is where the real power of it lies.

Motive is important too. The main difference between my past attempts at manifestation, and now, is the reason behind the desire to manifest. In the past I wanted 'it all'. My ego had a list of demands that tended to stick around itself, to help pad itself out and fluff it up. I desired money and fame as proof of success, to make life easier and more fun. Not terrible reasons, not evil, not even necessarily wrong. But clearly not right for me at that time, or any time maybe. These days my reasoning is more soulfully propelled. I want to manifest certain things so that I might fulfil my purposes. Although, if I'm honest, my purpose requires nothing to be fulfilled. I can pursue a hundred different purposes without anything. Because purpose, essentially is love and kindness. My manifestation desires focus around performing those purposes in relative comfort, and with less stress. So I want the same thing, but for different underlying motives and with a different input from me. That, it seems, is where the desire is granted or otherwise.

Manifestation, given all I have said, is about drawing, dragging the sacred into the profane. It is about recognising the divine within, accepting it, knowing that we are capable of all things when we engage with that divinity. The extent to which this grants your dreams come true relies on how far you go towards the divine within. It is all too easy to become lulled back towards the dirty, to become enamoured with attraction, to be human and desirous.

If we move, constantly and consciously towards a graceful dance with spirit, then our wishes have a better chance of being gifted to us. Although the nature of our wishes are bound to change when we fully become more aligned with our sacred being. So whilst we start out wanting a yacht, champagne and a billion dollars, the waltz with soul may have us downplay our desires to a riverboat ride, a glass of fizz and a hundred kisses. And that will be enough, because the cross-section of dirty and divine gifts us insight. Such insight is manifestation's only real goal. The gifts are but a lure, the bait that pulls us to see further and deeper.

HARNESS THE POWER OF PRINCESS OF PENTACLES

Explore the reasons for your desire. Shift them from 'I' focused and take a generous holistic approach. Ask not what your abundance can do for you, but what you can do with the abundance. How can the world be a better place through you satiating your material appetite? Who can you help today, even in the smallest way?

DIRTY & DIVINE SPELLWORDS OF PRINCESS OF PENTACLES

I manifest (. . .) for the wellbeing of my world.

KNIGHT OF PENTACLES

INTUITIVE MEANING

Get earthy and grounded in your desires. Plant your seeds and commit yourself to their growth. At the same time take life lightly, be jolly, be fun. Know when it is time to rest, time to work and time to play. Expect abundance and then get on with life. Don't stand around staring at your life expecting it to grow. Do what needs doing and move on. Trust that change has a way of bringing itself about without your interference!

This Knight is a fruitful, youthful representation of the male. He is a very gritty and real character. Think of the young men you see leaving school, seeking abundance, striding out to their first jobs. There is a willingness to provide, even if in their first instance just for themselves. Herein there is a natural balance. They work, they play. They work again. This is the energy of youth channelled into creation. It is the energy of creation, for creation's sake, and before responsibility (family, mortgages etc.) kick in.

MY JOURNEY

I'm not going to pretend the situation with my husband has gone away. Melted into the background, yes, but gone away, no. I think perhaps this is how we handle it. It has no effect on us until we have an argument, then it is brought into sharp focus. We can go weeks and months without such a situation arising. In the meantime, things are mellow. But there is always that danger lurking over us: is he okay? Is he feeling panicky? Is he drinking to cope?

I'm fairly assured that he is doing well, due to the fact we haven't had a cross word. That is the key indicator of his state of mind. When he is down, we fight over the silliest of things, usually instigated by him. Often it starts off as domestic stuff and lurches into all kinds of ridiculous territory. There is no reasoning with him when that happens. But it hasn't happened. All has been well. Which makes me nervous.

This time I am not for forgetting. I'm not ready to pretend everything is okay. Not when there is a bomb that could go off at any moment with all of us holding our heads saying 'duh, how did that happen?' Oh no, I'm no longer playing dumb to that particular vicious cycle.

So I'm in a state of hyper vigilance. It's exhausting. Alongside all my other mother stuff, and book writing, I have one eye on the beloved, a constant finger in his ribs, trying to keep him self-aware.

I wonder about other people's marriages. Many of my friends seem to suffer occasionally from spousal problems. I'm only getting a one-sided version, of course, just as you are of my situation. Then situations dissipate and everything is okay, for months, years, until something arises again. Are we all suffering in silence from the affliction of humanity?

When we meet a person, we put on a facade, a myth of perfection. When our weaknesses start creeping in, they do so under the guise of being 'charming'. How lovely that someone shared their issues with us, how romantic, how special we must be, how carefully we wish to cure and heal them. Then fourteen years down the line those same charming issues get old hat. The very things we enjoyed together in the early days, become stumbling blocks. People change, and then they don't change enough, or in the right way, and the world keeps turning and somewhere down the line we hold hands and other times we hold our heads in our hands proclaiming, 'why me, God, why me?'

Is this just life? Have I fallen for the Disney stench of romance, the falsehood that proposes a partner as being the stardust one needs to get through life? Have I really fallen for that shit, so that anything else seems unbearable? There is a lot to be said for fairy tales, for the way they show women. Yet I was reflecting on this the other day, thinking about Disney heroines and princesses. At least they are all portrayed as brave (even if in the pursuit of true love). They are all quirky, and, to an extent, intriguing. They may have impossible eyes, hair and waists, but they get to save the day, overcome evil relatives, offing baddies in their wholesome and beautiful wake. They get to learn and grow (to an extent). But the guys? The guys in Disney are even more decoration. Handsome doofuses whom the girls fall for indiscriminately, often just good looking guys who show up with a kiss and all is well. At least the girls get a part, a few lines, a motive. The guys are just fodder, background, some small inspiration. They are not protagonists, they are dumbass blokey beings: they are props.

That is what we are fed as youngsters. The female is the main emotional plot line, the dude sways to her whim. It's all crap of course. But right now I do feel somewhat Disney princess-ish. I'm the emotional undercurrent carrying the whole damned story line. My husband is the foppish, long haired counterpart who shows up and says a few lines.

The thing is, we make our own lines, we create our own stages, we value others how we choose. Perhaps I ought to bump my husband up to leading man status. Stop tickling his ribs with criticism and give him the stage, see how he handles it. I will step back, lessen my role, allow him to improvise with nothing but my support as guidance. I will intend and believe and trust that this is the better alternative.

HARNESS THE POWER OF KNIGHT OF PENTACLES

Look to how you create in your life. Do you load it with responsibility? Try shifting how you approach your 'work'. Do it today, with no reason attached. Do it because you want to, not because you need to. Explore that feeling. Work, create, be, for the sake of it, for the joy of it. Release the talons of need. Just do it, because you do. Then, at the end of the day, celebrate having done it. Work and play.

DIRTY & DIVINE SPELLWORDS OF KNIGHT OF PENTACLES

I release the script.

QUEEN OF PENTACLES

INTUITIVE MEANING

You can grow your empire. Whatever you want out of life, you can create. Every experience can serve you well, if you allow it. You can become a woman of the world in many respects and bring success to your own door. You can follow your passion and become comfortable within your own flesh and your material world: the beginnings of a powerful, worldly wise woman. If you ever doubt your ability, let that fade away now. See how far you have come. Look at what you have embraced and made work for you so far. You are a queen, know yourself.

MY JOURNEY

A day of ordinary. Took the children on an outing. Felt abundantly free to do so. I've been teaching my eldest how lucky she is to have the things she does. She parrots this back at me often, 'I'm so lucky, Mummy'. Or the other day she came to me declaring, 'we are rich, Mummy, rich, rich, rich!' A part of me wanted to correct her, explain that we aren't actually. But I didn't, because in time she will see that she has enough, more than enough, and that rich is something else, culturally anyway.

Simultaneously, in comparison to many, yes, we are rich. I will let her engage with that feeling as long as she likes. Combined with gratitude it does no harm. I will allow her our wealth, and I will grow wealthy alongside it. Because there is beauty in it. There should be no right or wrong in this. Poverty is a reality, and yet, there is enough to go round. We are as wealthy as we allow ourselves to be, if we simply shift our understanding of wealth, of being rich. So I will allow our wealth and my daughter's sense of abundance to just be as it is: simple, comforting, a seedling of her worth.

HARNESS THE POWER OF QUEEN OF PENTACLES

What are you wealthy in? Make a list. Revel in all that you have. Make that your fortune.

DIRTY & DIVINE SPELLWORDS OF QUEEN OF PENTACLES

I am wealthy.

KING OF PENTACLES

INTUITIVE MEANING

Accumulated wealth. Satisfaction in one's lot. Retirement taken to enjoy those things we have toiled for. The fulfilment of a working life. Aspects of the traditional patriarchal role such as being a provider, being a success at work. Creating your own world, building a home, providing for that home.

MY JOURNEY

I feel bloody awful today. I appear to have captured my daughter's sick bug. Rang my husband at work and asked him to come home. Coping with two little people is not such fun when you feel nauseous and have shivers running up and down your body. He came. He is my hero.

HARNESS THE POWER OF THE KING OF PENTACLES

You need not be in retirement, or a man, or even a provider to feel this card. What aspects of your life have you retired or satisfied? What aspects could you retire and allow to lounge on the good fortune you created? Indulge any abundance you have created, even if that is a few hours break from work. Make the most of it. Be the king of it. Know you earned it.

DIRTY & DIVINE SPELLWORDS OF KING OF PENTACLES

I indulge my ability to provide.

THE WANDS

The Wands (or Batons) are concerned with the element of air. They represent that which you cannot grasp, but that comes to you in the form of thoughts, inspiration, creativity and powerful solutions. They are the visions that set the world alight. They are the small ideas that make life liveable. They are the answers to the questions, all the questions. They are the questions too.

A philosophical, spiritual aspect of the tarot deck, the Wands are that unfelt, yet firmly understood, power of the mind, of the soul. I have little expectation for this part of the journey. Which is quite right, because, as you surely know, your mind, your heart, your soul, could speak anything, any time, any moment.

The Wands are the breeding ground for creation. They manifest whilst we prevaricate. They dare us, then they double dare us. We can choose to ignore them. That always feels easier, in the short term. Why follow our heart now, when we could do it next week, next year, next decade. . . ?

Society might prefer that we continue to ignore the fire of creation within. Because the Wands bring passion, and passion sparks revolution. Now that revolution may take place in your heart, in your home. It may spread its way out, rippling across friends, colleagues and Twitter buddies. Movements are sparked by the small notions that the Wands present.

The Wands provoke change. Change that starts somewhere deep inside. Not the kind that is sold to you, or the kind that comes in a jar. This is the change that the divinity within insists upon. If you ignore it, it rattles plates and throws fits and creates chaos. It may even force itself upon you, eventually. With a little internal insight and attention to who and what we really are, we can bring ourselves to the change long before it is actioned upon us.

ACE OF WANDS

INTUITIVE MEANING

The fresh steaming adventures of the soul starting to clamber their way forward. New thoughts and creative streamings bubble up, showing a new way.

MY JOURNEY

What the fuck is reality anyway? Following on from a good old fashioned vomiting bug I am now having an existential crisis. Not that I doubt my existence, on some level, I am most certainly here. But perhaps I doubt yours.

I feel like I'm in a bubble of self today. I'm rejecting all that I'm supposed to do/think/believe and wondering, in particular, why we all crawl up each other like a ladder of humanity taking us to A, B and C. None of it is real. I have this on good authority. I once had a dream/memory/vision which reminded me that none of this is real and I woke up laughing at how seriously we all take life. Not that it is unreal either. But perhaps that it isn't The Thing. And The Thing is what? I don't fully know. I know it's better though, different, less real and more so, all at the same time.

The thing with The Thing is that we get glimpses of it and we take them ever so seriously. Because enlightenment is no laughing matter right? We must renounce all forms of hilarity and brevity and swap them for some high pull gravitas. We must mantra, chant and strike poses that fiddle our way forward into a more spiritual way of being. Never alluding to the fact that The Thing doesn't give a fuck about all of that. Because it's not fucking real. Our perception of The Thing is as unreal as anything else. All the while The Thing may well be real, but in its wake it spawns nowt but misunderstanding, calamity and highly crafted confusion.

I'm not approving of my use of the F-word right now. But then none of this is entirely real, and so my disapproval is phoney. So is yours. We all have the right to a pure page of paper free from curses and decorated solely with poetry, beauty and ravenous wordings. But that's fucking crap too. I'm all about the F-word now. Our disdain for it arises through a set of beliefs, and beliefs stem from thinking. Right now I'm pretty convinced that everything we think is generally two bum shuffles away from crap, maybe less, it depends what you ate.

So what is real? That depends on you. Certainly very little that you have ever thought is real. Those things you learned and the advice you take, that's not particularly real either. Your house, your shoes, your business meeting and your car. That's just fodder to give your day some kind of structure.

There is nothing wrong with the unreal either. Don't get me wrong. I'm surrounded by the unreal. It is very comforting. It becomes problematic though, when we start to believe in it, when we invest ourselves to it, when we follow it blindly.

That's the malady of our times right there, the challenge for our species. We invest ourselves in the unreal, so badly, so deeply. We torture ourselves with it. We become it. We dress and garnish our lives with it like pepper and spice. We cling to it like a recipe for elusive happiness, following set steps as outlined by Delia or Nigella. Yet because it isn't real it crashes every so often. We wake up in the night, sweating, cold, horrified. *Shit, this isn't real,* we realise. Come morning we wake, fuel ourselves and surrender to the warmth of the unreal over and over.

Perhaps if we engaged with The Thing a little more, and opened ourselves up to the fact that all is unreal, we may find a form of comfort in that too. If everything is a facade, a myth, an unreality, then you can't go far wrong. If all the advice you have ever followed is somewhat crap, then you may make your own path, taking as guidance only what arises from your heart. When life is unreal, there are no mistakes. When life is unreal, then being guided by love is enough. When life is unreal and we look to The Thing for guidance, then maybe we find ourselves. Not other people, not textbook answers, not an education, not a lesson, but ourselves. You aren't fucking real. Take that as a compliment.

HARNESS THE POWER OF ACE OF WANDS

Pursue unreality. Anything that is not yet formed, explore it. Whether that be an idea, a feeling, a creation, a new recipe... Take something that as yet is not in existence, and give it life. Watch how your heart, mind and hands can toil together to make a thing which previous to your inception of it, didn't exist. Feel this conjuring. Apply the feeling to life!

DIRTY & DIVINE SPELLWORDS OF ACE OF WANDS

I follow The Thing. I have faith in The Thing.

TWO OF WANDS

INTUITIVE MEANING

Stuck in one place, dreaming of another. There is ambition in you that has not yet been fulfilled. It haunts you. Be confident that all things happen for a reason and in perfect timing. Try to focus on your current place in life and learn absolutely everything that you can from it. Let ambition drift away for a moment and focus on the here and now.

MY JOURNEY

It's easy to talk about unreality. Yet it's difficult to live within it. As much as life may be a part of something more, it's not something that particularly matters when faced with sickness, trauma, fear and death. Those things don't marry well with a blush of unreality at all.

So it was as I stared at my young daughter all day long. Hand constantly upon her brow measuring for the state of sickness, worrying about what to do next. Two months of illness have set me on high alert.

To break the tedium and to create some semblance of control over our lot, we booked a holiday. We are off to Bulgaria, the Black Sea. I like the sound of that. A dark expanse of liquid sited in a mass of land that is Europe. Complete with never-ending food, a choice of beds to minimise the 'foot in face' snugness of co-sleeping and several ancient churches and historical sites for me.

I'm so excited. I'm buying straight into this particular unreality and it feels good. I'm making the most of it. Isn't that the point? To believe all this craziness with a full heart and to embrace it, to find joy in it? Right now I believe in Bulgaria and I believe in a green crochet swimming costume I have my eye on. I believe in passports, border controls and currency. I believe it, not because it's true, but because it makes me smile.

If nothing is real, then reality is crafted by where we choose to place our faith. That faith manipulates time and space and compels creation. It is The Magician's greatest trick, making us invest in that which is not there, and shifting us so that we truthfully experience it. If in the end none of it was real, then the only thing that matters is whether we enjoyed the illusion.

HARNESS THE POWER OF TWO OF WANDS

Choose something unreal to get excited about. Be it an ambition or a day trip. Invest your whole self into it. Get into the myth and allow it to give you purpose, smiles and excitement.

DIRTY *&* DIVINE SPELLWORDS OF TWO OF WANDS

I believe in my joy,

THREE OF WANDS

INTUITIVE MEANING

Perhaps you feel that you have been 'called' and whilst you might not know precisely what your calling is, or where it will lead you, you have the foresight of an explorer, excited yet sensible, and ready to take on new challenges!

MY JOURNEY

Last night I went to bed hungry. Usually my sleep is quick and fuzzy, sedated by a full stomach, but since having a sick bug I haven't wanted to eat.

When I did fall asleep, I had an interesting dream.

I dreamt the world had ended and everyone had died. As this happened nothing changed, except perhaps the light. The light shifted, the focus altered, like an Instagram filter was added. I was separate from my husband at the end of the world. He was elsewhere, yet we had a conversation that went a little like this.

'Are you still alive?'

'I am.'

'Are you different?'

'I am.'

'Are you the same?'

'I am.'

Then I woke up only gently aware of how profound that was.

The phrase 'I am' was not plucked wildly from the ether. I recently listened to an interview with Wayne Dyer who repeatedly trumpeted the phrase, in its Biblical entirety (Exodus 3:14), for self-growth and spiritual understanding, 'I am that I am'. It hasn't much left my head since then. It echoes around my edges and has in time provoked a serenity within me. It is acceptance and power all rolled into one.

(I might add that 3.14 is the number of Pi. Pi is the number of chaos. Chaos is beautiful, it creates all. So within chaos is, 'I am'. If we wish to take it further, who we truly are, when this life is done, is an exodus from chaos... I'm just playing with words here. But I like the effect. Meaning is, after all, where we find it.)

I am all. I am nothing. I am this. I am that. I am alive. I am different. I am the same.

HARNESS THE POWER OF THREE OF WANDS

What are you right now? One word. Take it. Be it. I am...

DIRTY & DIVINE SPELLWORDS OF THREE OF WANDS

I am the same. I am different.

FOUR OF WANDS

INTUITIVE MEANING

A card that tends to represent engagement, marriage and commitment. The roles described are very traditional, and the couple are celebrating being together, each adding unique but complementary talents to the love-in. Perhaps not having a great deal yet, but certainly having each other and the beginnings of a future. There is the promise of possibility. Lots of potential here. If you are in a relationship this card reflects gentle contentment with old fashioned gender roles. If not, then this would represent a dear hope.

MY JOURNEY

Some things you can fix, change, manipulate and manifest. Other stuff just hits and splatters your heart with shit.

My baby daughter was found to have a kidney anomaly when I was pregnant. I prayed, I asked others to pray. It seemed all was well. She is well. She is a massive, chunking child. She is blossoming and blooming. Her health remains seemingly unaffected by whatever is within. As a result, I called a halt to the invasive tests that were so stressful and upsetting for her. I manifested for her to be okay. And she is.

Except she isn't, maybe. Having read some more about her situation, and tallied that with what I have observed, she perhaps has a problem. One that is directly related to her condition, and that as a mother I can't write off. My prayers kept her safe when in utero she was labelled with a potentially fatal cyst. My prayers were answered when I asked for her to be clear of all the various genetic issues that the doctors said she had a high chance of having. My prayers brought her to me: a great big bundle of snuggles.

Perhaps when I see it like this I know that I have been dealt the easiest of many possibilities. Maybe, because of my prayers. Yet, one of the possibilities seems to be coming true. Out of my control. Nothing my manifestation wizardry can either challenge or change. It is as it is. The stuff of life.

I stopped the medical train and in the end, it is I, the least qualified, who has had to dig deep and admit to the potential diagnosis I see in front of me. Will that excuse her from a battery of tests? I hope it may. If it doesn't though, at least I can hold her hand and tell her I prayed, and that in the end, when life happened, I held it again. That I always will. That no matter how unwanted a situation. No matter how hard we mitigate against it with every cell in our body. If it happens, I'll hold her hand. Sometimes that is the only manifestation right we get. And I'll take it. A million times over, I'll take it.

HARNESS THE POWER OF FOUR OF WANDS

Accept your lot. Cease the fight. Hold hands with whomever needs it.

DIRTY & DIVINE SPELLWORDS OF FOUR OF WANDS

I accept this and hold it with love.

FIVE OF WANDS

INTUITIVE MEANING

Life may feel like an uphill battle. Others' opinions may crack against yours causing fractures and misunderstanding. The best you can do is express yourself from your truest passion and allow others to put forward their perspective. Remember that we all are coming from different situations and our intentions, desires and requirements can be so different. Fight your corner, be heard, but ensure you listen too. Be calm and stand your ground and with this approach agreements, stalemates and maybe even peace can be reached.

MY JOURNEY

I'm broiling in the irony of all that has befallen me on this *Dirty & Divine* journey: the irony and the agony. Spirituality is beyond the ability to create. It penetrates everything. As I have worked through this journey I have found enlightening thought and internal change arising. Relationships are subject to flux and change. Careers and cash are up for renegotiation on a whim, by the wind. I got comfy in all those parts of me. I slathered myself in all their possibility, their frustrations, their bullshit. All of it, totally in my power to change, accept, be with and decide upon.

I easily got what I needed. I got my holiday. I got comfortable and then life knocked my skittles down. That is the magic of spirit. It never stops giving. Good and bad. It never allows you to hide for long behind the nicety of modern life. It will take your vision board and rain lava upon it. Hot blistering soul saturating lava.

I received everything I wanted on a superficial level. Then I had space to see some truth. To see beyond an illusion that I'd effectively sold myself. Magic will get you there eventually.

Spiritual practice is not about bringing things to ourselves. A divine connection is about so much more than fulfilling our surface needs. Yet we bargain with those needs as if they are the (only) bridges to soul. Those surface needs that feel fractious are surprisingly easily healed. This allows us a foot into a spiritual life. It has great value. Though it is a salve over a wound that requires stitches.

The wound was never that we need more. It is that we don't see that we are enough. So we distract and we use our power to furnish our bathrooms, and we believe that we are the Priestess of Water. Then the real flood comes and we can sink into spirit or spit it out into the tumult like a worn toy.

In creating sustenance for our hands, hair, feet and home we grade ourselves as spirited. Which we are. Always. But there is more. There are the depths we avoid plumbing. Sickness, aging relatives, daily monotony, the fucking stinking fear. That which most tests you, that is where your spirit is at. It's the heart wrenching, terrifying, inevitable and yet somehow beautiful truth.

That is where I find myself now. Bubbling against the truths this *Dirty & Divine* journey is hastening my way. What else is going to rise up? What other aspects of my life are due for an honest airing? Where am I due comeuppance, restorations, healing and recuperation? What other illusions have I single-handedly created that need to be blasted into the past to make way for what should be, what is?

It is what it is. It always is. And what it isn't, won't stick. My glue has melted, let life slide back into place.

HARNESS THE POWER OF FIVE OF WANDS

The fight is keeping the wolf from the door. What if you simply opened the door and let the wolf in? Try that. Try giving over to the inevitable.

DIRTY & DIVINE SPELLWORDS OF FIVE OF WANDS

I drop my barriers and allow life to come in.

SIX OF WANDS

INTUITIVE MEANING

Remember your successes. This card asks you to see how far you have come, further perhaps than many people expected. This card can represent someone who has been dealt a difficult blow or a rocky start, but who carries on regardless.

MY JOURNEY

I'm beginning to think of the Wands as the wounds. All great things stem from the pus filled injuries of our past, do they not? Of course they don't. Love creates great things too. Yet love's great things are easier, they are more passive. Love pats you on the back and keeps you motivated. It's the ache and the pain that drives us the rest of the way.

What is the ache? The ache stems from a primal need to connect, to exist, to be seen. It's a spiritual need too. It's a social media speciality. But it means nothing without touch, intimacy, empathy. Without reality it is just concepts. So social media gives us a feather of connection, but we long for a wing.

I feel a little lonely today. I'm not alone. Maybe I am just fed up. Maybe I just need another coffee. Maybe I need to get out of my head, out of this house, out of the doldrums.

These days are blending together. Merging into an amalgamation of sniffles and sneezes. I won't remember this time much. I will remember that my baby said, 'Mama.' She said that three days ago, and not so much as a peep out of her since. Perhaps that is all I will remember. Even if I decorated these days with great journeys, adventures and thrills, it would all slip too easily from memory.

We invest so much in the creation of life. Then forget it all anyway. Sometimes I think we do too much. We are a people separated from need. Because we don't need anything, we aren't required to lose ourselves in pursuit. We have water, food, shelter, clothing. We are provided for. Our lives become, instead, a search for entertainment. All equally forgettable.

Sometimes it is nice to just stop trying. Yeah, today I feel a bit blah. I'll go with it. I have some seeds to sow, some plants to grow, literally. A bag of salad seeds and some pumpkin plants that need potting. Today I'll lose myself to that. I'll let all that has occurred within me in the past few days pass into the soil. I will send it to the goddess because for now that is my only power.

Oh, and I will clean the house. Because that is what I do. In lieu of having to do anything else, my primal function, for this moment, is cleansing. On all levels. Removing the muck, creating space, moving on.

HARNESS THE POWER OF SIX OF WANDS

Take your day as it comes. Shift with whatever attends you. Allow yourself to grow through the day.

DIRTY & DIVINE SPELLWORDS OF SIX OF WANDS

I take what comes with grace.

SEVEN OF WANDS

INTUITIVE MEANING

Sometimes life is an uphill battle. Other times you are stood at the top of a hill, fending off attacks and difficulties from what feels like everything and everyone. You may currently feel drained by several sources. Everyone wants a piece, everything is taking your energy. You are not sure if you can carry on at this pace, feeling like you are constantly fending things off. Here is the thing: you can and will cope. Make time for you, stay grounded, be around things that bring you joy and that keep your feet firmly on the floor. Don't allow the stress of the situation carry you away. This phase will pass, and when it does you will see a myriad of learning and strength gained from it.

MY JOURNEY

The sun is shining and doesn't it seem true that whenever the weather picks up so does our mood, events, situations and understandings? My daughter got into our local school today. I have mixed feelings. Though a part of me, in this sunshine, thinking back on my school years, feels pleased for her.

There is a part of me that wants to rebel, to create my own reality wholly and without exception. The world of others isn't good enough. Then there is the conformist within me, who has lived in the mainstream and found it to be perfectly fine, better than fine at times. Being a fence sitting Libran I straddle these two aspects of life, my inner life and the one I am actually living, and I struggle to decide which is better. Perhaps neither is better. Perhaps the balance is the key.

For nobody can take my reality, simply because I am subscribed to another. That is where worlds collide and when life gets interesting: the moment we open to the reality of others. Whilst school may be a corporate, government entity, it is filled with many other souls, those of teachers, those of pupils, all bringing their reality to the table. Just as my daughter takes hers forward with her, to share with those who are lucky enough to cross her path.

She is an exceptional friend already. She has her heart set on every child she meets or sees upon the park. I remarked to her recently that she was naturally a 'friend maker'. She looked me dead in the eye and said, 'No, Mummy, I'm a love maker'. And who am I to argue with that? Let her spread her love far and wide.

As the sun warms my back, I let go a little, allowing my love to be the only pull towards me that she needs.

Speaking of the world's colliding and varying realities, I have just been perusing the internet. I was chilled to see the powerful images of migrants escaping the wars in their countries. When I say chilled, I mean I physically felt like I was placed in the freezer aisle at the local supermarket. People disembarking tiny vessels stacked high with women, children, families. Women, despairing, homeless, country-less holding tight onto their beloved babies. Men weeping with relief laying flat out on beaches, having made it some of the distance towards whatever they hope for and away from whatever chased them.

My flesh crawled with the absurdity of my first world problems. Shall I school my daughter or home educate her? What privilege I have. An actual choice. There are human beings, the same as me, perhaps better than me, traversing oceans to try to provide a life for their children. A life. Not a pissing education. A life. They are trying to keep them alive by risking all they have. By risking their lives.

Reality is an awkward thing. It vcers so suddenly from your own, to that of another. From this perspective we can weep and wail our lot or we can wonder in awe at what we have received. I'm going to choose awe.

HARNESS THE POWER OF SEVEN OF WANDS

Where does your reality fit into the reality of the constructed world around you? Where does it rub? Examine how you feel about that which is yours, and that which is forced upon you. As the worlds collide, focus on the good that comes from this collision.

DIRTY & DIVINE SPELLWORDS OF SEVEN OF WANDS

I collide into new worlds with passion.

EIGHT OF WANDS

INTUITIVE MEANING

A blast of exciting fresh and creative air is headed your way. It may show up in a number of ways. It isn't a threat to your current way of life. Rather it is complementary to it. Embrace and make the most of any offers and opportunities. This fresh wind is set to stir things up and make life interesting. Count your blessings and expect only the very best. Ride the energy and enjoy! Making the most of this time will help new aspects of your life emerge and unfold. So trust what arises and go with it!

MY JOURNEY

Today was a blast. It started with bickering last night, that carried through to taint the air sweetly. Sincerely, sometimes an argument clears the air, it brings people back to a common sense of togetherness. It tightens bonds by reminding us that those bonds require maintenance.

Today was sunny. We ate ice cream and swung on swings, we found a friendly horse and a set of stepping stones. We had little adventures. We got outside of our ordinary. We discovered things on our doorstep that were new and life-infusing. It was just a fabulously lush kind of day.

The crud fell away. It was replaced by butterflies kissing my daughter's head, my baby grabbing her feet, my husband and I being together gently and with presence. Simple days like this are the point.

HARNESS THE POWER OF EIGHT OF WANDS

Get lost in something simple. Enjoy the easy life. Whatever makes you warm and cosy, try that.

DIRTY & DIVINE SPELLWORDS OF EIGHT OF WANDS

I accept the simplicity of joy.

NINE OF WANDS

INTUITIVE MEANING

The careful use of one's skill and achievement to negotiate the way forward. Trust in what you have learned and allow it to buoy you up, without necessarily having to place it on the table to be seen. Nothing needs proving. You have the necessary ability to walk whatever tightrope presents itself.

MY JOURNEY

My husband took a day off work and we all went mountain climbing. Or that is what it seemed. Where we live there is a beautiful country park with quite a hearty hill smack in the middle of it. From this site you can see all across the county. It is simply stunning. We set off with our three-year-old, and the baby strapped to my chest.

I was impressed with myself. I got up there whilst carrying a six-month-old who weighs a stone and a half, barely breaking a sweat (barely). For a woman who hasn't exercised in a year or so, that was good going. Most impressive though was the effort made by my three-year-old. She walked the whole distance, from car park to hilltop, without fuss, without needing carrying and with good humour. She only has little legs. She usually accosts my husband to carry her on his shoulders before we reach the end of our street. So to clamber her way up what is effectively a mountain in her world, was unexpected.

This shows to me that we can achieve anything we put our mind upon, so long as we want to and as long as it stays fun. We ensured that the whole lengthy trip was entertaining for her. She gazed in awe as the view expanded the further we got. She simply loved the pleasure of being with us all as a family. I strode on ahead, we sang marching songs, we examined deer faeces, we jumped over springs bubbling up from the ground and we clambered up rocky outcrops. Each step was an adventure.

There is a life lesson here. Don't stare longingly into the distance and then trip over your own two feet. Skill and achievement are only gained by sticking to the path right ahead, the soil literally beneath our feet. Looking ahead to the future only makes it seem further away. Getting your head down, placing one little foot in front of the other, brings that future up to meet you quicker than you expect, and without the stress. Every second can be a worthwhile part of the trip, if only you allow it to be. It helps too, to occasionally look back with pride, to gaze in amazement at how far you have come.

HARNESS THE POWER OF NINE OF WANDS

Live second to second. Cut short thoughts of the future. Focus for the day on what arises only.

DIRTY & DIVINE SPELLWORDS OF NINE OF WANDS

I am this moment.

TEN OF WANDS

INTUITIVE MEANING

You might find yourself overwhelmed. If that is the case then try to share the workload, or simply reject things you do not need to do. You are in control of what you are responsible for. Make wise decisions and allow yourself room to move, to breathe and smell the flowers. Do not become so overburdened with tasks that you lose sight of what you really need. Shake it all off and make time for you!

MY JOURNEY

I was woken by the dawn chorus. In my bedroom. The varmint cats had brought a poor bird in. My husband stumbled out and wrapped it in toilet roll. He thought it was dead, but apparently it recuperated. As I lay in bed waiting for the alarm, all I could hear was the birds continuing to sing outside. It felt forlorn and tragic. That goddamn circle of life. How dare it intrude on my sleep and bring me back to its chilly reality?

When you are outside and you hear a bird sing, it echoes out into the universe and you don't realise quite how loud and reverberating that sound is. When the noise wakes you from sleep, signalling fear, a cry for help, and the bird's voice bounces back off the four surrounding walls, it is another world. It is like nails down a blackboard, only more pitch perfect, more cloying. Correct that, it was like nails down my soul, pulling the innards of grief out.

A little later I rose and was greeted by cat vomit spiked with feathers and guts. The same bird? I hope not. It seems cruel that we rescued her from her feline fate, only for me to be scooping her up an hour later.

Needless to say, it wasn't a good start to the day. It has continued in that weird vein, somewhere between dawn and dusk. I have felt assaulted by decisions that I won't bore you with the details of. I've had two tired children, making that fact known with their chirruping voices. I have shuffled myself to the whims of everyone else and back again. I smelled burning on the stairs, I developed a headache, I type this surrounded by housework, not quite able to juggle a broom with my desire not to.

The oven just sneezed, perhaps it too is coming down with a case of 'can't be bothered'. Sometimes there is just a blur of things to do, situations to think about, decisions to be made. I am very much with the Ten of Wands today. Back laden down with wood, or in my case, letters and bits of paper, errands and forms. It's all piling up around me like an uncomfortable nest. Between that place, and the chilling birdsong that woke me this morning, I am bereft. The light has flown; the sunshine of the past two days has departed. I miss my husband. I surrender to the gloom, to the mist of the TV light. I will allow it to pull me in and I hope that along the way my to-do list takes care of itself.

HARNESS THE POWER OF TEN OF WANDS

Whatever is breaking your back, weighing you down, acknowledge it. Look to your life and list those things that are cramping your style. You don't necessarily need to do anything about it. Sometimes acknowledgment alone will kick-start the necessary self-awareness to slowly pull your time and effort in happier directions.

DIRTY & DIVINE SPELLWORDS OF TEN OF WANDS

I look up and away from my burdens.

PRINCESS/PAGE OF WANDS

INTUITIVE MEANING

This card represents a whole host of new opportunities. You are being asked to get in contact with your deepest inner child. Perhaps you left her behind a long time ago, buried her under adult life. Well, she is back, and she wants to play. She has creative ideas and inspiration to bring to your table. She is asking you to see the world differently, from a younger perspective. She wants to shake things up and get zany. The zanier the better. Consider what you left behind in childhood. Who were you, what did you love, what made you happy? Find that part of yourself once more, and invite her out to play. Make her a dish of her fave grub and dig in. She never really left you. She has been waiting. Open the door to all the fun and wisdom she has to offer!

MY JOURNEY

This card brings my thinking on reality back around. This time, though, my feelings and thoughts have been centred on authenticity. It's 2016 as I write this and so many celebrities are dying. Prince was the latest, passing just a few days ago. Alongside this and in particular the death of David Bowie, I've been left thinking about personal truth. Which of course is a shifting thing.

When I became pregnant with my second daughter I had just begun to emerge from a three-year period of hibernation after having my first. Whilst I felt ready to spread my wings and become a little more me again, the universe within my loins had other ideas. So I put my ideas of self to the side, again, and embraced pregnancy and the world of baby.

Having a second child has solidified my personal idea of self as a parent, as a mother. Whilst previously I felt it was a hiatus in self, I see that, for now, this is my self. I am all about being mama. I do enough on the side, such as writing this, to have a little something just for me. Yet, right now, the most of me is mother.

That's my authentic truth. For now. The Princess of Wands stares in confusion and wonder at the wand in her hand. Today I wonder what she is thinking. She seems to have been given something, and doesn't quite know how to incorporate it into her self. Perhaps it is a skill, a talent, or maybe a label. I wonder if she is being asked to go against the grain, to go against all she has known. I feel that she has gifts to share with the world, and that finding a suitable way to do so can be overwhelming.

My answer is this: forget the critics. Do what you love. Life is horribly short. To be authentic we must create from within and not give any thought to what anyone else thinks about that creation. We must shift with the light, as it illuminates different parts of our inklings. We must explore our own possibilities, constantly. If it doesn't feel a little scary, a little testing, then we aren't digging deep enough. This goes for everything: love, friendship, work, hobbies and everything in between. To access our authenticity, we must get uncomfortable. From here we can break the moulds set around us, and become more ourselves.

HARNESS THE POWER OF PRINCESS OF WANDS

Create your reality, follow your dream, ponder the meaning of existence. Challenge yourself, your heart, your mind. Take something a step further.

DIRTY & DIVINE SPELLWORDS OF PRINCESS OF WANDS

I welcome the challenge of my creativity.

KNIGHT OF WANDS

INTUITIVE MEANING

Passionate, fiery and full of your own power. You have used this for causes, thoughts and people you believe in. Though at times you may have burned bridges. There may be a reckless element to your strong beliefs: slinging arrows before perhaps having learned all the facts. Though this isn't all bad. You are a defender and a fighter, with good reason too. Sometimes it is lonely to be the only one brave enough to speak up. It can lead to isolation as supporters drop away. Most important though is that you honour your heart.

MY JOURNEY

My husband has a severe migraine and I am just pottering on. I went to a birthday party for a little boy whose naming ceremony I performed back when he was three months old and I was heavily pregnant. His mother came over and told me how much something I had written was helping her. What I'd said was that we must cease the search for an outward achievement and just be in the moment, embrace our current purpose. She had finished a business she was trying to run and was just focusing on her boy and immediate situation.

I confessed that I only post what is pretty much relevant to me. That I am, too, just doing the necessary, accepting each daily purpose. For the time being. It will all shift again. She will be a successful business woman one day I am sure. I will dedicate proper time to writing, not as I am now, with one child on my lap and singing across the room to the other.

We get on with what we need to get on with. Sometimes we fight against that, and in doing so, we make life difficult. Other times we accept our temporary situations (all things are temporary) and we give our best to it. The fight is not worth it, and usually becomes a battle of the ego. When we get past that, life flows a little better. Whilst resignation to the moment may feel like stagnation, if we keep a dream in our heart and work towards it, even if only in fantasy, then we are still moving, dreamily, spiritually, towards it. Our purpose is never the end of anything else. It is always, simply, a stepping stone to the next thing. As I have said before, we don't have a purpose. We are a purpose. Let purpose rush its way through you at its own speed, and in its own way.

As awkward as my literal life is right now. Typing with a blonde head constantly bobbing in the way of the keys. And that same blonde head asking when it is her turn on my computer. And I'm trying to type this whilst explaining that this is Mummy's work. In the end I hand the computer over to her. And I tell her this. 'One day you will read this book and you will know that Mummy wrote it with you on her knee.' From here my purpose is embedded within my other purpose and awkwardly they twist and tumble me towards the next thing. Never a pain, never a problem, always a challenge, forever cosy, snug and a tight fit.

Okay now she is starting to pat my fingers up and down as I type. Message received. Purpose calls.

HARNESS THE POWER OF KNIGHT OF WANDS

What are your most fervently held beliefs? Not ethical or moral values. But your personal beliefs. What do you stand up for when necessary? What gets your blood boiling? What subject/s could you rant on for day upon day? These subjects choose you to be their champion. Think a little on how you might further advocate for them.

What action have you taken in the past for the things you believe in? Perhaps sometimes it has been helpful, perhaps other times not so much. Weigh those actions and reactions and make conscious choices for how you might better represent your beliefs in the future.

DIRTY & DIVINE SPELLWORDS OF KNIGHT OF WANDS

I honour my passionate beliefs with the wisdom they deserve.

QUEEN OF WANDS

INTUITIVE MEANING

This Queen is full of creative longing. She is at one with her life, her situation, her ability to transform and grow. There is warmth, wit and humour about her. She is grounded and connected to herself. She makes the most, often spectacularly, of her lot in life. She finds sweet fertile soil where others only see stinking cow dung. She loves to create and to bring forth etheric gifts, making them real and tangible within the physical sphere.

MY JOURNEY

This is my card. I always pull her when I need reminding of myself. She is my Queen. On my best days I am her: a woman in her creative power.

Today is not that day.

The theme of sickness roars on unabated. My husband is beyond himself with a migraine. It's bad. I usually accuse him of man flu. But this is visibly wiping him out. I am, for now, a single parent. But, of course, it's not that simple. Halfway through the day I came down with an upset stomach. All of this compounded by both girls issuing sneezes with each breath.

Sickness has dogged this tarot journey. What I had hoped would be a dramatic revival of fortunes has become an inner experience fuelled by dependence, tissues and coffee. That is clearly how it has been meant to be. Being ill, and having an ill family, has kept me small. I have been left to marinate in my own being, and much of my journey has depended upon that for learning. It has allowed for very few real world interactions, and sparse as they have been, they have nevertheless added weight and value to my inner experience. This theme of sickness, tiresome, exhausting and at times worrying, has ignited my inner resources. It has been a beacon of self, showing my capabilities.

Destiny does not always show up in shining lights and six inch heels. Sometimes she creeps in the back door, showing up as the mundane, the dreary, and the dire. In this quiet, boring surrender we may find aspects of ourselves we hadn't recognised. Yes, you might climb Everest to test your metal, but it may be more realistically plumbed over a three-month period, stuck in a house, providing for others. One is more glamorous. Each, though, provides an insight. If you allow it.

I wonder how your journey is? I am so curious. Are you going within, or perhaps you are enjoying a frisson of good health and taking your quest outside for a walk? My journey is far from what I hoped. Yet it is what I needed, I trust that. I hope, with my

Queen of Wands crown on, that my example is providing good fodder for your journey. I suspect it is showing in glaring ways how spiritual, intuitive understanding comes not from success or instant manifestation, but from the gritty bowels of your existence, perhaps literally.

HARNESS THE POWER OF QUEEN OF WANDS

What is challenging you? What is your recurring theme throughout this journey? Consider how any blocks may in fact be allowing for greater understanding.

The Queen of Wands is creative. Stand back from your immediate situation, look at it from an objective situation. Allow yourself a moment to comprehend your situation as part of a tapestry of life.

Aim for creative expression. Maybe you will add extra ingredients to your dinner. Perhaps you will doodle across your latest electricity bill. In whatever small way, bring art to your day.

DIRTY & DIVINE SPELLWORDS OF QUEEN OF WANDS

I welcome my blocks;
I allow them to raise me beyond expectation.

KING OF WANDS

INTUITIVE MEANING

A kindly, inventive and quirky King. He is the hippy dad with unexpected thoughts and astonishing insight. He doesn't rear up all potent and omnipotent, like some of the other kings. He sits wisely with quiet and calm. He comes when ushered and brings along with him vats of potential and knowing, which he shares gladly.

MY JOURNEY

I have a confession: I have a new way of spending my time. In between acts of motherhood I have very little time. Literally thirty minutes a couple of times a day, if I am lucky. I should say that I am spending that time invested in a yoga sutra or perhaps meditating. But I'm not.

I have downloaded a farm game app on my phone and I love it. There I said it: I love it. It is a great little space saver for my brain and I refuse to feel shame. It is, for now, what it is. Why am I confessing this now? I'm not sure. Maybe to show that I'm human. Yes, I am managing to write a book whilst baby naps, and run a household. But when that downtime hits I'm not sipping green juices or running barefoot hunting for pansies. Oh hell no, I'm squeezing bacon out of pigs and growing (probably genetically modified) soybeans on my pixelated farm.

It is fine on our spiritual paths, our dirty and divine paths, to hustle ourselves away and indulge some next level reality. Whether that be a book, a film, a soap opera, or a farming app, it is essential to take that time out of our existence and for a few moments, be something other, someone else.

In my everyday reality, I'd love to have a little small holding. Never would I squeeze a pig of its bacon, but I could keep some chickens and a pet goat. For now, I enact the fantasy in cyberspace, which has little bearing on anything true. Yet the truth is not what I'm lusting for. What I'm needing, here and there, is five minutes to just invest in something that means nothing, that wants nothing from me, that doesn't get frightened or die or cry if left to its own devices.

What does this have to do with the King of Wands? Truth? Reality? Unreality? It's all meat on my bones. I sit here, an ancient and wise soul, endowed with a voice to express and share and seek. I sit here goddess-like, sleeping cherubic child at my breast, finishing up this sentence before I reach for my smart phone and interface with my growing crop empire. There is no contradiction, only truth.

HARNESS THE POWER OF KING OF WANDS

Go do something else, something worthless and unspiritual. Know that your wisdom and spirit will not fade or decline as a result. Give yourself a break. You are spirit, you binge watch Netflix, you read the Daily Mail website sometimes and flick straight to the celebrity section. Go be you. Indulge the vapid side of life. It's okay. You are okay.

DIRTY & DIVINE SPELLWORDS OF KING OF WANDS

In my wisdom I am nothing. In nothing I have wisdom.

THE SWORDS

I left Swords till last because of all the suits they are ones I least get. They remind me of maths. I never liked maths. I don't know why they remind me of maths. Hard lines and unforgiving edges perhaps? Let us speak no longer of numbers and equations.

The Swords are a suit that make me nervous. Flick through the images on your pack and you will see why. They are not pretty. They speak of disaster. Though of course, nothing is truly a disaster, it all twists into something beautiful, eventually.

The Swords are also strongly masculine. The Sword is a weapon used by warriors and soldiers. It is an item whose purpose is to bring death, or perhaps, serious injury and disability. It is made to create success, at the very real expense of someone else. Its noble purpose, to protect, to defend, is tainted by the fact that any defence comes too via the blood loss of others.

I'm wishing I had done this suit first, got it out of the way. But I didn't. So this is perfect. Let us pound out this last suit with high expectation. The Swords will slice through our old, dead and hazy, to bring the final taste of clarity on this *Dirty & Divine* journey. The end is nigh. Let us be grittily enlightened.

ACE OF SWORDS

INTUITIVE MEANING

You are being given a glimpse of something, but not the whole picture. There is more. Perhaps you have the start of an idea, but no idea of the details. Follow the leads like a detective and allow a fuller picture to arise slowly and over time. A fascinating time full of intriguing, mysterious potential.

MY JOURNEY

Well, the health issues reached what I hope was a pinnacle over the past 24 hours. Last night my husband, through lack of sleep and exhaustion caused by the pain he is in, went totally delirious. I found it funny for a moment, until I realised it was horrible not funny. His mood swung wildly from elated to anxious, panic to hysterical laughter. All over the course of an hour or so.

I remember hallucinating and becoming delirious as a child. It was hellish. I hoped I would never revisit that again in this lifetime. But to have a grown man suffering under the same delusional, fever-induced thinking is a little scary, a little funny, and a lot sad.

I had to take hold of him in my arms and rock him as I would a child. I stroked his head and repeatedly told him that he must sleep. I called him 'little one' and I hushed him gently. He fell asleep. Only to wake minutes later, wild-eyed and confused. In the end I had to leave the room. My presence, was not as calming as I'd hoped. Me being there provided an outlet for his feverish paranoia. So I gently left, encouraging him to sleep.

He was sent as an urgent referral to the hospital eye clinic today. After last night's mental gymnastics, he was worn out and worried. I was worried. I don't usually worry. Lately though, with all the repeated sickness, trips to the hospital and ambulances, I was a little afraid.

Some awful thoughts went through my head. How do I explain this to my little girls? How do I engage my positivity with disastrous ill health? How do I cope? What song was it that he said he wanted playing at his funeral? How do you cancel a holiday? You know those kinds of thoughts. The ones that are too easily entertained.

Let me cut to the end. He is fine. As ever. He has a migraine. As suspected. Yet the mill I found myself in churned itself into a foamy fluff. I'm coming down from that now. I am left asking what we should learn from all this.

We must see what is before us. That seems to relate nicely to my husband's eye situation. I will share that hippy wisdom with him later. We must give over to whatever our health is ushering in. And it does bring forth messages.

I have come to some very stark realisations as a result of this spate of sickness. It has challenged my perspective on who I am and what I am doing here. It has given me clarity on so much. It has made me a different kind of mother. It has brought me life back. After several years of nursing and being in a cocoon of baby, I am ready to step out and into a flush of youth, with all its energy and optimism and health. It's time to draw back the shades and just live.

I am allowing the universe to open up not only for me, but for us all. I am relinquishing control. In this week my daughter was given her school place and immediately her world is flourishing in new and spectacular ways. The universe is carrying her. I don't need to be her all.

Her life, outside of the cocoon, is beginning, and it is beautiful. The release for her, for me, is a relief and brings me closer to her in all new ways. With freedom comes love, not with ties. She is little, she is full of laughter, I believe the cosmos wants to hear it outside of these four walls.

Another situation has turned and transformed these past few weeks. I was in denial regarding my little baby's kidney issue. I called a halt on certain tests. Now I'm in no man's land with no real knowing of whether she needs further help or not. So

I am engaging with those tests. My mama bird instinct was to keep her in the nest. Yet again, and because of health, I am allowing the nest to widen, to become a community of nests, all of which want to cosset and protect her. I'm entering the reality of community, because whilst my reality is nice, it needs flavour, it needs guidance, it needs to trust that there is wisdom found in the feathers of others too.

Finally, the other thing that has changed, is me. I bought a whole stack of new clothes. I got sassy with myself. I haven't really bought clothes in years. Only the odd bit here and there, mainly pyjamas or scruffy house and pregnancy clothes. I treated myself to some new threads that help me feel more like me, and less like a shadow of someone I used to be. It was a charming little trip into inner change via the mirror: dungarees, dresses and an awesome pair of wedges.

It's been a hell of a trip. This tarot journey has brought me closer to my own life. I hadn't recognised my own refusal to budge. I had formed a view of who I was, and what I was doing, and I was sticking to it. *Dirty & Divine* has powerfully removed me from my own sticking points. It has shifted me into a place of acceptance and helped me to see that by letting go, we don't release, we receive. What we receive is often what we thought we didn't want. What we don't want can be the most needed thing, the most incredible.

HARNESS THE POWER OF ACE OF SWORDS

This is the last curve of your trip. What has changed? From this new stance what do you hope to glean from the rest of this journey? A new intention and hope may be relevant. Revisit what you want from this. Craft a new beginning with anticipation of only two things: growth and change.

DIRTY & DIVINE SPELLWORDS OF ACE OF SWORDS

Through growth and change I become.

TWO OF SWORDS

INTUITIVE MEANING

Life is scary. We have no control, not really. The map we think we tread, is, in fact, rather precarious. It isn't as well-trodden or inevitable as we hope. We are one step from falling spectacularly into turbulent, abject failure at any moment. What keeps us safe and dry is faith. Faith that the sun will rise, that we will make it through the day alive and well. One day that faith will be misplaced. Yet we have it anyway. We must. Apply that to those things that you invest with fear and allow it to carry you through, foolishly faithful till the end.

MY JOURNEY

Everything is unknown. That which we fear. That which we hope for. It is all subject to the perversity of some unknown force, or forces. Today has been a random day. I have followed my nose and gut about, undertaking errands, and spur of the moment side trips. As a result, it has been interesting. By following my feet, with no expectation, I've had many mini events happen. The universe offered a slice of life.

Honestly none of it is worth sharing here. Yet it was all good fun, all very unexpected and, I suspect, just the start of new things. New friendships. New habits. New ways of being. New ventures outside of the house and into the world.

It is amazing what can be tossed your way, when you choose to simply turn up. We cannot ever know what the next moment holds. All we can do is walk on into it. If we do so openheartedly interesting things happen. It is inevitable. There is power in accepting the nothing of everything, the everything of nothing, and just doing your day.

HARNESS THE POWER OF TWO OF SWORDS

Follow your gut. Make no plans and be pulled. If you feel an urge to take a shortcut or, perhaps, a longer route, just do it. If you are compelled to leave early or stay later, just do it. Allow the wind and your mood to tumble you towards whatever destiny happens to have in store for you. Move and see what happens.

DIRTY & DIVINE SPELLWORDS OF TWO OF SWORDS

I am always headed towards the divine.

THREE OF SWORDS

INTUITIVE MEANING

Heartache and heartbreak. Plain and simple. The residue of past pain that still reverberates, still feels fresh. The heartache that made us. The suffering that, to an extent, defines us.

MY JOURNEY

I can think of three heartaches in my life, in the traditional romantic sense. They occurred when I didn't want to let go of something that wanted to let go of me. I think, perhaps, that is the definition of heartache. The pull of your heart towards another, (romantic or otherwise), when they have already taken out the scissors and cut the strings. Ouch! Yet we keep on mentally, emotionally and sometimes even physically, attempting to revisit that lost situation. Spiritually we place our soul in the care of someone whose soul has moved on. We don't get it. For a while. Perhaps we move on. Perhaps a small fragment of us doesn't, not ever.

Is there a solution to this? Maybe not. Maybe we are meant to scatter seeds of our souls to the spirit of others. I wonder if we collect pieces of others too: those that have lost their hearts to us just as we disregarded them — wrong shoes, bad hair, ugly temper. . .

Heartache, like genital warts, is for life. It's not a bad thing. It is the stuff empires are built upon. I bet all great visionaries harbour a sliced-up heart. From here they were catalysed to do something, anything, to show their worth, to show the rejecting party just what they released.

The people who broke you, who they are, what they are, is mainly a creation of your mind, and what they allowed you to see. That which you mourn, is to an extent fantasy. Twenty years tied to that party may not be as lush as your heartache-riddled perception believes.

There are other heartaches too: death, disaster, missing pets. They all leave us changed. Without them we may not feel the burn of our purpose. Yes, heartache has its reason. It does marvellous things with us at the same time as it fells us to ashes.

HARNESS THE POWER OF THREE OF SWORDS

Think of one heartache you have endured. Call it into your knowing, just for today. See how it influences your perception, your reaction, your understanding of self. At the end of the day release it back to memory. See what you learn.

DIRTY & DIVINE SPELLWORDS OF THREE OF SWORDS

From pain my heart expands.

FOUR OF SWORDS

INTUITIVE MEANING

Rest, relaxation, recuperation. Reignite your tired soul by taking some time out. We need not always be on the edge of doing. Sometimes the best thing to do, is to do nothing. To consciously and purposefully stop, close the door, put down the book. Sleep.

MY JOURNEY

I won't piss and moan about the continued state of health in my household. I will say this though. Baby got a fever. Baby cut a tooth. The medical authorities strongly deny that fever and teething are related. Ask any mother: teething and fever are related.

You know what you know and sometimes the world, the authorities, know nothing.

If you take time out and focus on the task in hand, and you learn something, and the world says, 'No, you are wrong.'

I say, 'Forget the world'. Intuition, be it women's, or mothers', or just plain old intuition, knows its truth. Giving it space to arise is all it needs. And it will come.

HARNESS THE POWER OF FOUR OF SWORDS

Gift yourself permission to relax, rest and recuperate. Sleep, eat, meditate and dream. Finish a good book. Gaze at clouds. Do whatever it takes to switch off.

DIRTY & DIVINE SPELLWORDS OF FOUR OF SWORDS

In peace I meet myself.

FIVE OF SWORDS

INTUITIVE MEANING

A card that signifies the fight, conflict, betrayal and war. What is being fought for? Who is winning? How have you lost? What did you lose when you won? This card can link into our cockiness, and our ability to walk our talk. Are we being arrogant? Have we left others sore and wounded as a result of ambition? It is a card of success, but the main question is: at what cost?

MY JOURNEY

I figured out something about myself today. I stumbled upon it whilst mopping the floor, and it shook me. I stopped, I looked up and said 'Ouch!' I believe this journey, this *Dirty & Divine* path, is what provoked the reckoning. All these days of introspection, compounded by the inability to do very much, has had me delve deeper than I realised. It bubbled up, as the steam from my mop rose. There, I met myself. I met the baby me. I met the pain I didn't know I carried. Ouch!

I have always felt a loner. I've had friends. Yet I've always felt different. In more recent years I have shunned the path of many and become quite proud of my alternative self. I am not so alternative that I stick out like a sore thumb. I straddle the midland and the 'other' rather well. Yet inside, I have always felt odd. I have grown to be proud of all that is peculiar about me.

Now this oddness came about rather suddenly. Of course it stems back to childhood and I can pinpoint the moment. I can pinpoint the words I said. It was only today though that I realised just the weight they carried.

I was six or seven years old. I was happy. I thought I was famous. My dad was the local vicar. The world was mine. There was nothing not to love about my life. If there was discord in my home I was oblivious. Then my parents came to my bedroom and told me that we were moving house and that Daddy was going to live somewhere else because he was a writer.

I remember feeling desolate. I remember my main concern was leaving my Brownie pack, leaving my school, abandoning my friends. I loved those things. I was inherently part of them. I had a place in them.

I have never had that since. Not that same way. Since this moment I have always felt odd. The new girl. The girl hiding something to pretend to fit in. The girl embracing the alternative because she was different, wiser, than everyone else. The girl who won't get on board fully with groups or communities or schools of thought that require much of her.

I always thought I was different because that is what I believed myself to be. It was what I loved. But in fact being different was part of surviving, it was who I became after I lost my early happiness. I realised today that the happiest time of my life was when I was a part of something, connected, tribal, intimately a piece of the scenery. And the thing that struck me, that made me feel pain, was not that I have been too cool for school. But rather this: I reject groups, communities and membership not because I'm better than them (as I have thought), or my ways are so very superior (as I have believed), but because I don't want to be lost from them again. I've become a lone wolf in response to that very first major loss. It's so sad. It answers to my everything right now. It's the root of all my things. It's the angle upon what I have become turns.

I'm not saying that my alternative beliefs or ways are bad either. They are just fine. I like them. They are important. They have led me to interesting people and interesting places. I have opened to all manner of intriguing thought and I have lived a little outside of the usual, the norm. At the same time, they have led me into trouble. I studied Women's Studies at university, which was the most eye-opening, shocking, tear-inducing journey. Though at that same time, my inclinations led me to the dark band of stoners whose music and social life was vampiric and draining (and much fun and an experience).

All things have a purpose. My alternative living led me to my husband. To that music lifestyle, to the party living, to a refusal to grow up or get serious. Which is glorious. Was glorious... For a long time now I have been trying to escape that. I did. I just stopped. But again I was alone. So my loneliness led me inward, shunning all of that and becoming a spiritual hermit. Me, my cats, my writing. No regrets, never regrets, but certainly it is time to move with a new mood.

Then I had kids. And my eldest carried on with me, we became breastfeeding radicals. I went against every grain I could find. I became her shelter. I was keeping her safe. But then baby two came along and things shifted again. Daughter one got older, I am no longer really enough. Circumstance wants me to put my solo self away and to reach out, to enter the norm a little, to stop being so damn afraid of the world and get on with straddling it, intimately, truly and with purpose.

I have found that I'm missing a piece. The piece of me that wants community, that once loved community, the part of me that was more a part of the world, easily and naturally. That little girl within, the one whose life shifted irrevocably, she wants back in and she wants to play out, not alone, but with others. She wants to be a part of the local furniture again.

I guess it is no big surprise that this has come up. Having children is inevitably turning me towards community and being a part of something other than myself. Spirit is grand, spirituality is a wonder, thinking differently is a gift. But people are spirit and maybe I ought to remember that and fall headlong into some circles, tribes and packs. If we are all spirit on an essential level, then community matters. If life is where I find my spirit, then becoming a part of the life of others, and they of mine, is essential.

I attended a local fete today. We have lived in this village for two years and the fact that I recognise faces used to make me cringe. I would shy away from connecting beyond what was necessary. Today, for the child inside me, I embraced it. On the way home I spoke animatedly to my eldest about my love for Brownies when I was her age. I got excited, genuinely. Particularly because I can give her that simple gift of community, and all being well, it won't be taken away from her.

I used to consider that the break-up of my parents was good for me. It humbled me. It showed me another world. And yes all of those things were benefits. But had I not been plunged into the world of 1980s lesbian motherhood and pagan goddess worshipping fatherhood, would I be that different? The answer to that question is irrelevant. I would have become myself eventually. Indeed, I'm probably not quite there yet. I hope to have many years left to shift into the better version of me.

Today's discovery has been a big one and it came from seemingly nowhere. It leaves me with something to do: I must explore community and make friends. I will become a part of something again, wholeheartedly, without cynicism or being removed. I will allow myself to experience whatever that brings. I am fearful of this. Something in me expects doom, or, at the very least, vanilla boredom and gloom. Yet I will do it all the same. This is the next step of my journey. To greet the alternative that exists in us all and to quit making myself so damned different or unusual. To be me, amongst others.

HARNESS THE POWER OF FIVE OF SWORDS

What is your inner contradiction? What should you do, but your habits rail against? What is the fight that is stirring your soul? If there is a conflict within then consider it relevant and important.

Sometimes we close down our empathy and become unnecessarily defensive. Drop the pretence. Walk yourself slowly past the walls you are placing in front of those things you see as difference. Become that difference, try it on for size.

DIRTY & DIVINE SPELLWORDS OF FIVE OF SWORDS

I move through the block of fear and allow expansion.

SIX OF SWORDS

INTUITIVE MEANING

The crossing between then and there. Difficult change, and yet, worthy. An essential journey that may in part feel forced. Though perhaps that force is a little dose of divine guidance.

MY JOURNEY

I just looked ahead at the Swords that are left and I'm wondering again why I left this suit till last. They are dark. The outlook, on paper, is morose. I'm hoping my experience will provide a different depth to this. That's the thing with the cards, they can look scary, but the multi-coloured reality of that is actually quite different. It is always unique. You may see a man with ten swords in his back, but how that plays out in life will always be something a little special. So I stumble on. . .

If I thought life had gotten a little lonely, then this week has gone on to prove that further. Husband has gone straight from a migraine to tonsillitis. I'm left still holding the kids and running the house. It's been remarkably fine. I miss the company of another adult. At the same time, it's been a charming break in itself. I see how I am as capable as I'd ever hope to be single-handed.

The husband has been taking active steps to become healthier and happier. It's a slow burn though. Every little disagreement we have feels pivotal. I love him, sober and sane. When he isn't, he becomes difficult to be around: I like him much less. Whilst all has been relatively well, we aren't there yet. It's like having two husbands. One is kind, funny, handy and thoughtful. The other emerges less often, but is small-minded, grumpy, anxious and petty. I utterly deserve better. But then most days he is better. Most weeks he is better. That is why it is difficult. That is why people don't just up and leave people.

The patriarchal powers though have us all digging in for perfection. Anything less than perfect is ultimately deemed disposable. In this day and age, we have to fight for our weakness, for our fallibility. We look to partners to save us. We look to partnership to be a boat upon which we merrily float through life. Humanity is not that boat. We, all of us, come loaded and shot through with fault and failure. The challenge for each of us is to vision our way past our blocks. Every block tells a story. Every block can be upturned and made a step stool. Only, though, if we allow it.

That's where I find myself at, between the crux point of perfection and imperfection. I find myself swallowed and treading water between my husband's strength and weakness. Herein I find my own strength and weakness. All of which is unpalatable to a masculine society that only accepts male power and female acquiescence.

Here I must disembark the cultural thinking on love and perfection and follow where my heart leads. Even when, sometimes, my heart feels utterly ridiculous. It has a voice. One that is empathetic and sympathetic and annoyingly tolerant and forgiving.

The image on the Six of Swords is very much how I feel: guided, blind, through a sea that I cannot navigate alone. Trusting that the end of the journey is ahead, that there will be dry land and illumination.

So I continue on. Happy. . . most of the time.

HARNESS THE POWER OF SIX OF SWORDS

Where are you on your journey? In what area of life do you feel lost and at sea? Give over to the gentle flow and ask your guides and angels to carry you forward. Release the path to the goddess and allow her to sweep you forward.

DIRTY *&* DIVINE SPELLWORDS OF SIX OF SWORDS

I pause with trust in the natural flow.

SEVEN OF SWORDS

INTUITIVE MEANING

Losing oneself to the fear, anxiety and regret of the past. You may feel like you are sneaking around uncertain, worried what others think. You may not feel ready or wholly qualified for certain aspects of your life. This card speaks to those fears and tells you this: you will never be ready if you wait to be ready. Do not let the past define you.

MY JOURNEY

There is something stirring inside me. I can't put a name on her. She is rising up, she is calm, she is potent, she is powerful. I bought new dungarees. Yes, dungarees. For some reason when I put them on I feel all kinds of wonderful. I'm wearing them a lot. Today I have felt like a referee, fending off everybody else's bad moods.

So I hitch up my dungas and strut about. Since when did dungarees make a girl feel wild and sexy? I'm not sure what that is about. Maybe the dungarees are a symptom of something bigger. Maybe sexy isn't lace undies, but the freedom to dash around without our clothing getting in the way, falling off or peeking above our trouser line.

The sun is shining and I feel ready to burst into or out of something. The internal dialogue is hot with things I shan't share here. Unformed thoughts that are rebellious and grown up and mature and frantically feisty.

I feel more myself. The younger, wilder version of me is around. I feel her. Except she isn't quite herself. She is exhilarated in her flesh. She is objective and rising out of an essential feminine essence. I'm feeling Isis, I'm feeling Kali, I'm feeling Bridget. My divine women are riding waves of goose pimples through me, and I'm listening, waiting, being with them, intrigued by where they want to surf me to next. *I am here*, I say. *I am here*, I feel. *I am here, I am.*

I feel like I'm finally moving, charging towards something. I don't know what. I don't even care. The charge is the thing.

These are some damned powerful dungarees!

HARNESS THE POWER OF SEVEN OF SWORDS

How are you deceiving yourself? Allow truth to arise to your surface today, in whatever unexpected format it presents itself.

DIRTY & DIVINE SPELLWORDS OF SEVEN OF SWORDS

I plough through my own deception.

EIGHT OF SWORDS

INTUITIVE MEANING

You hold the key to your freedom, but you are so wrapped up in anxiety, fear and self-doubt you cannot see that. You are all you need to escape any situation or unhappy thinking. You must unwind the emotions that hold you back and stop the limiting thoughts. There is a bigger picture here and you are at the heart of your life. Already life is asking you to release, and your wellbeing depends upon it.

MY JOURNEY

Today has been harrowing. It started last night with the baby screaming and crying and unable to sleep. It went on throughout the night. She couldn't breathe properly and kept waking in fits of hysteria. I've been lucky. I've not had that with either girl before. I'm exhausted. Thoroughly wiped out. A terrible night's sleep was compounded by my tonsillitis-ridden husband snoring like a series of sonic booms. So when I woke at 4:39 to a still screaming baby there was nothing I'd rather do than leave the house. Though the destination, Accident and Emergency at the local hospital, was not my ideal hotspot.

I'll cut the story short. She is okay. She has a virus, a wheezy chest and a snotty nose. I have dedicated the day to her. Allowing her to use me a bed, food source and shoulder to cry on.

I feel absolutely emotionally floored. I'm physically drained. My spirit has hit the deck.

I found myself railing at spirit a bit today. The catalogue of sickness, whilst not so serious, has been hellish. I'm not upset it happened. These things do. Yet I feel deprived of spiritual comfort during all of this. I haven't had any soul food. I've stumbled on, searching my heart, mind and soul, but without a lot of magical coincidence or spiritual signatures being left.

It's not that I doubt a spiritual entity. It's just that one hasn't shown up. Not that I've noticed. All the coincidence and thoughts I've had in this book, are brought forward from my brain, my intuition. Which is, in the main, how a soulful understanding is sought, through our own inner experience. But at the same time I would love a little spice and magical wonder to help make this past three months go away.

Maybe I'm not seeing it. Perhaps I have to look harder. I suppose the fact we are all still standing is gift enough. I asked for a holiday: it is forthcoming. I asked for book writing work: the deal is nearly done. I asked for health: none of us is dead. I asked for money and my bank account is sufficiently full. I asked for my husband to get himself together and he is doing, slowly, but most surely. Am I being ungrateful? In the face of all this is it selfish to expect a little slice of soul?

When I started on my spiritual path I was inundated by coincidence, wonder and awesome events. My life, for a while, was orchestrated and brought to me by all things otherworldly. I was visited by signs aplenty. I'm short on them right now. After the day and months, I've had, I'd really just love a little heads up, an etheric high five. Just something to warm my heart, make me smile and say, 'yes, I'm here.' I'm known, I'm loved, I'm doing okay.

HARNESS THE POWER OF EIGHT OF SWORDS

Ask for a sign. Put yourself in the way of the universe, shout and wave and ask for it to reveal itself back. There is no harm in asking for a little love, something tangible, something unique, just for you. . .

DIRTY & DIVINE SPELLWORDS OF EIGHT OF SWORDS

I expect love.

NINE OF SWORDS

INTUITIVE MEANING

Comfortable mourning. All is well in life, more or less, but you still feel down, maybe a little low. Even, in spite of all you have, and all you have achieved, there is a tendency to feel a bit less. Rest, give some special time to yourself, prioritise your basic needs. Know that rest is essential, not a luxury.

MY JOURNEY

Last night I had an unexpected heart to heart with my husband. Or rather, he did with me. His recent irritability, sickness and his long term issues have collided and he has brought a confession to the table. He is an addict. It's not a new confession to me (or you). Normally it comes after a huge argument (usually over the dishes). It goes away and vanishes, as a few days later he justifies the odd beer here and there. And I, cynically but willingly, go along with the facade.

This time the admission came peacefully.

I've always said he isn't a drunk. That he drinks for comfort and to plough down stress, like so many other people. Alcohol is a the most legitimate drug around, and one that storms through lives invisibly and with government approval. The occasional tax hike is the lip service to the fact that, it may be, in fact, dangerous and deadly.

Do I think there is any hope? Well, he took himself of his own free will and without my knowledge to the doctors and was referred to an alcohol specialist team. So that is something. We shall see. The hope I do have is not in his direction any more. What lifts me up is the fact I know I can do all of this alone. And for the stuff I can't do, or don't want to do, I can draft in any number of helpers, paid or otherwise. I am more than capable. As Whitney said, 'I'm every woman,' and a couple of dudes too.

So I continue to be in this situation until a time as it gets better or becomes unbearable. I've done the supportive love. I've done the threats. I've done both of these intermittently and over years. Neither actually work. Nothing I do will prompt him to fix himself. He must prompt himself. He must want that fix.

So yeah... The Nine of Swords. Trapped, trapped, trapped. The only way to escape is to see my own power. To follow that. Nobody holds me hostage except myself.

HARNESS THE POWER OF NINE OF SWORDS

Where are you trapped? Pull the string and see how it unravels. Who is the keeper of the string, the key, the lock? Is it you perchance? You hold the sword in your hands, is it time to cut yourself free?

DIRTY & DIVINE SPELLWORDS OF NINE OF SWORDS

I release myself.

TEN OF SWORDS

INTUITIVE MEANING

Death of self and personal enlightenment. It is that big. Crisis of self. The Ten of Swords is potentially the darkest looking card of the whole pack. Its image — death, destruction, murder — is deeply powerful. When a part of us dies, we open to a complete new life. This is what this card represents, the total metamorphosis of being. It is the butterfly of the pack. The caterpillar must cease to be, to allow the wings to unfold. You must cease to be, in a very real way, for the next part of your journey to take flight.

MY JOURNEY

I have my dungarees back on and I'm stomping forward. I woke to a happy baby. The freedom of which is palpable. To have a healthy child. Thank you, goddess. She is still being treated for various minor ailments. But she is smiling. The empowerment in this is vital: I am alive, she is alive. The sun is shining. I have the day stretched out ahead of me and boy, oh boy, does it feel good.

On the other hand, my husband's migraine/tonsillitis has shifted again and he is now vomiting and complaining of stomach pains. Add to that a big dose of exhaustion, and possibly depression, and that pretty much sums up his dark cloud. I'm not sure what to do about that. Nothing seems appropriate. I'd pray for him to raise a smile. But that's his cross to bear and his prayer to make.

That aside, today has felt something special. We went to a friend's house for tea and cake. We were surrounded by wonderful women and half a dozen little girls. We talked, we commiserated, we had things in common, unexpected wonderful things. Things that made me feel less alone. Things that made me feel sane.

It's lovely how connection can bring us back to ourselves. It's beautiful how health and blips in it can remind us of life, of who we are and what we want. Today I feel utterly myself. A brighter version of that which I can sometimes become. There are four cards left in this journey, and whether there is a happy ending ahead I don't know. Today, in its own weird way, feels like a happy ending. Not because I fixed my marriage, or even my baby daughter's ongoing health issues, not because I had any resolution of any kind. It felt like a happy ending because I am in my own skin. I am in my own heart. I am in my own mind. I am in my own spirit. It's not a compromise. It is very much enough.

As for signs, things to make me feel warm and cosy inside, I was watching a program on alcoholism. The baby started to cry, really, really cry. I paused the TV to hold her and try to decipher how to help. Next time I looked up I saw the TV was paused on an image of the Virgin Mary and baby Jesus. An image which I have no idea how or why it was related to the show I was watching. But one that I managed to capture. It felt relevant, it felt nice.

That paragraph was just interrupted by my husband coming down in a state that I didn't expect. He is basically having alcohol withdrawal. Something I told him he shouldn't worry about, as I naively believed he doesn't drink enough. Clearly I know nothing. He drinks more than I know about, that much is now obvious. So I just took him up a beer, babe in arms, and told him that this is it. It doesn't get lower than this. Needing to drink so badly that his body freaks out and shuts down if he doesn't. That is shocking to me. That rocks my world and not in a good way. The misery within wants to ask how I ended up in this situation. The happy in me sees this as a sign, I finally have the truth, I can now know the dark depths of this situation. It's not just a habit, it's a physical need, a disease. It doesn't make me any more forgiving. It raises my hackles. It changes things. Though as yet, I am blind to what I do next.

You know that prayer I didn't make. I'll turn it in now. I'll pray for me. For my daughters. That this finds a resolution. One final thing: I feel better. Because for once, right now, I can see the extent of this problem. The truth will out.

Secrets and lies, people, secrets and lies. Yet, I still feel fabulous. Nobody can take that from me. A shadow has been cast but I will party in the shade. All of the above is as it is. And what comes next. There is a storm outside, perhaps I will be struck by lightning and gain a shamanic superpower. Now there is a plan. . .

HARNESS THE POWER OF TEN OF SWORDS

Get powerful in yourself. No matter what ends. You are always granted a new start, a new powerful you. Feel her tugging at your heel, let her in.

DIRTY & DIVINE SPELLWORDS OF TEN OF SWORDS

I am always the new me.

PRINCESS/PAGE OF SWORDS

INTUITIVE MEANING

What an awesome little transformer this gal is. She hasn't always got a clue what she is doing, but she has a heart full of courage and a head full of possibility. And, by goddess, she is moving through the dark, fighting through the glare of day, making way for herself in a messed up world.

MY JOURNEY

I've removed my emotions from my husband's situation. I am listening. I'm not making judgements. I am no longer trying to fix anything or anyone. I'm making space for my husband to say what needs to be said and then figure his way forward. He has taken the necessary steps without me, as he should, and he assures me he wants to change his situation. I am stepping back and letting him find the path he needs. Not the one I think he should take, but the one which is inevitably waiting for him. The path that waits for us all when we choose, mindfully and sincerely, to slay our demons and move on.

Relationships are the stuff of dreams and nightmares. Over the path of this journey I have witnessed the worst and best of my relationship. The good rubbing frustratingly up against the bad, till we can't see the truth of it for all the murk. Yet today I just see his situation as his.

And mine as mine.

I wonder where it will go. Our paths, merged as they are, and yet so entirely separate, are dancing around one another unsure. I've no energy for the negative. I've no desire to be subject to his moods any longer. I will simply step back, into my own power, into the safety of my own arms and I will observe.

This tarot journey has unearthed so much. Not just for me, but for those close to me. It has been a raw and potent magic that has brought painful blisters to the surface. Am I so arrogant that I believe that my undertaking this tarot journey has affected my family? Well, yes I am. I may not have made my children sick, or my husband an alcoholic, but I have reacted and acted, under the influence of the tarot, in response to these things and life has shifted as a result of my intention and what I have opened. The ripples are cataclysmic. This is my doing. I am that powerful.

It feels somewhat like I have opened a portal into the darkest energies in my life. This tarot journey has brought the grit truly to the surface of our beings. From here we are faced with questions on how to heal ourselves. How, and if, to accept others. How to accept and pursue my truest desires. How to make sense of the madness, the big picture, the little picture, the life we are living. This is a life examined and it is fabulous and fucked up in equal measure.

As for me. I feel more whole. I have exorcised a great deal in this journey. Salt has been rubbed into wounds, which has stung, but provided the beginnings of a curative effect. Herein I am finding my divine. From the dirt, the pus, the muck, the mud, something miraculous grows.

HARNESS THE POWER OF PRINCESS OF SWORDS

What has your *Dirty & Divine* journey caused in your life? Take responsibility. Know you are that powerful.

DIRTY & DIVINE SPELLWORDS OF PRINCESS OF SWORDS

I am that powerful.

KNIGHT OF SWORDS

INTUITIVE MEANING

Determination against confusing odds. Fighting through a storm. Finding sanity within the fog. Showing up even when the situation is frightening. Becoming a force of nature to position oneself against the winds of life.

MY JOURNEY

I woke to a cheerful husband. He is consciously making efforts to be sunny. Which is nice, if nothing else. Last night he nearly ended up in an ambulance on his way to hospital. His stomach pains grew worse and he lost blood when he went to the toilet. All things have consequences.

He remains determined to get help. I was thinking today of the journey we have traversed this past few months. It started early on with the death of my husband's friend. What I didn't mention then, was that that friend was a severe alcoholic, and that is essentially what caused his young death. That much had always been inevitable.

When that friend died my husband, quite logically, declared an intention to cease his problem drinking. Quite illogically, and as life tends to go, he has apparently done the opposite. Those big things in life, the things that shock us into rehab, into self-exploration, into healing, also sometimes make our demons stronger. Perhaps those demons need to visit their full force upon us before we can truly see them, before we can call in a priest. Before we can be the priest.

And then this. . .

An hour ago my mother-in-law called me up. I thought it was for a running update on my husband's bowels. It wasn't. She had bad news. My husband's dad has cancer. Of what type and severity, I couldn't gauge from her. He is having an operation very soon. I broke the news to my husband. There is no such thing as bad timing in the battle of life. When faced with mortality, again, we either dig deeper into our devils or we renounce them once and for all. Last time the devils won. Another chance is being offered, the angels are calling. May they be with my husband. May they be with his dad.

On another note, and to mark the keen intermittence of life and death, I just spent the afternoon at a one-year-old's birthday party. This particular one-year-old is my good friend's daughter, and she was born quite significantly prematurely. It has been a hellish year for their family. The little girl's start in life was incredibly difficult, enduring operations, transfusions, resuscitations and illnesses amongst many, many other indignities.

My friend has suffered. I cannot imagine quite how deeply that situation would scar a heart. Happily, though, this tale does not end in woe. She is a bouncing, happy and occasionally bad-tempered little lady! She has railed against her lot and is thriving. It was a lovely party, a celebration of overcoming all those odds. A celebration of life.

HARNESS THE POWER OF KNIGHT OF SWORDS

Plunge forward into the contradictions, the life, the death the melody that flows in between. Embrace the chaos. Dance, sing and fight through it. What you do, doesn't matter. What matters is that you do.

DIRTY & DIVINE SPELLWORDS OF KNIGHT OF SWORDS

I do life. I do it all day.

QUEEN OF SWORDS

INTUITIVE MEANING

This Queen is free from the silliness. She knows the truth, and she honours it, even if it is only an intuition. She reverberates with the moment and releases control, worry and vexation. She is organised, timely and ridiculously perceptive. She understands you don't need her, you need yourself. She keeps her energies tight and pungent. In this she is free.

MY JOURNEY

Today feels like a 'getting things in order' day. I've thumbed through a stack of paperwork relating to everything from ballet lessons to mortgage payments to tax. I'm trying to be organised.

At the same time, I have a cunning plan to go visit Grandpa, if he is well enough. Last night he had nurses out administering morphine. He says he has a small patch of cancer, that it is going to be cut out in an operation next week. My husband says he thinks he is downplaying it. He went to visit him yesterday. He just turned up unannounced.

Grandpa told my husband how he had retrieved some baby fish from the mother fish's mouth and kept them in a separate tank, so they don't get eaten by the other fish. My husband related this to me with tears streaming down his face. This is a terrible situation that I think will now forever be echoed by birthing fish. I can't even find anything more to say about that. It's just what it is. Baby fish and cancer.

So what else did I do on this day of Queen of Swords? I started reading a great book, in the sun. I chased the tortoise round the garden to prevent her numerous escape attempts. My husband came home, baby was asleep, we made love.

Which is an unusual thing in itself. My libido since birth has been zilch. Our connection has been frazzled, no doubt, in part, because of that lost link. That is one thing in a myriad of life situations that doesn't help. We also managed some time for a chat. He is ringing about new jobs. He chased the doctors regarding his referral for his alcohol situation, he visited his dad again. All of this without my instruction.

I started this journey as a search for the feminine divine. She hasn't shown up in a vision or miracle. I am beginning to understand where she is though. She is me. She always was. She isn't a saint begetting magic and rainbows in her stead. She is the ability, within myself, to cope, to stride on, to support all kinds of calamity with grace and potency. She is the steel in my soul. I may moan, she may moan, but underneath that fine mist of complaint, lays an infinite source of strength. With that I hold it all together.

Under the Queen of Swords, the feminine divine takes on a new guise. She is about the immediate. She relinquishes control of others and allows them to navigate their own paths. Her concern is with that which she can manage and control, and she isn't confused by what that is. She is self-aware, and at times, cold. But her chill is not through lack of love, it is through the knowing that she is not the boss of your world, only of her own. She knows when to step back and force her kids, her husband, her friends, to walk without support.

She cuts unnecessary cords so that she can invest her energy only where it is needed. She doesn't leave people helpless, she leaves them in their own ability. She is no mother hen. She is a mother fish, she spits her babies out and swims away. She trusts in an omnipotent force, such as Grandad, to keep them safe. Shit, Grandad is fish god, fish midwife, doula of minnows. If Grandad, (who spent time locked up with the Krays), and who is an utter bloke (with as many dodgy qualities as charming ones) is a god, a doula, then by golly we all are.

HARNESS THE POWER OF QUEEN OF SWORDS

Cut your cords to anything which no longer needs or appreciates your attention. Take a moment to silently envision cords tying you to different situations. Picture yourself taking a pair of scissors or a samurai sword to those ties. Send love to the situation, send thanks, send trust, then chop, chop, chop. Release yourself.

DIRTY *&* DIVINE SPELLWORDS OF QUEEN OF SWORDS

I cut dependency and allow growth.

KING OF SWORDS

INTUITIVE MEANING

Who or what is your authority? What is the truth of your world? Do you look to a smart suit or a drum-beating shaman for your sanity... or yourself? That which you are presented with, the obviousness of existence, is all myth, it is an act in a play that you didn't write. The real truth, the ovary-deep honesty of life, lays in you. Strip away rules, regulations and 'common sense'. Delve deeper, somewhere secret. Ask yourself, what do I really know? Become your own authority.

MY JOURNEY

This is it. The last day of the tarot journey. It has a glorious, ominous feel. Anything can happen, though it probably won't. The devil, as I have found through this past 78 days, is in the detail. My eldest daughter just sneezed, twice. Here we go again. I go forward armed with vitamins and swords in my breast. Bring it on King. Let us finish this thing well.

True to the above nothing much happened. Whilst I had hoped to bow out of the journey with a bang, it was not to be. The only thing of note was walking in the rain. I haven't walked for any long period in drenching rain since my teens. I was born in northern England, and it rains a lot: proper bone-soaking, cold, glorious, powerful rain. Rain walking with a broken umbrella (whipped immediately inside out by the force of the heavens) was standard in my youth. Since moving to the Midlands I have found the weather meek and mild.

Today I got sodden. My intact umbrella sheltered the kids. I took the full force of the torrents. It was dripping off my nose like a broken drainpipe, I needed to towel off when we got home. I loved it. Whilst many would moan and drag the kids full speed to the nearest shelter, I allowed them to stay dry whilst I indulged the downpour. It felt very real.

This journey has been real. What I wanted from it — miracles and adventure — have been eclipsed by the rain of reality. The cards have hijacked me back into myself, down from the clouds, and landed me in a puddle of self. Here I have met all that I am, all that I allow, and who I'd like to tweak myself into being.

Life is a very real storm. Sometimes we fight the ghostly wind of our minds. Other times it is the tunnels and furrows of the landscape we are mired in, reshaped by unseen forces, the movement of the plates beneath us, the explosion of lava turning our hearts to stone. No woman is an island, she is more, she is a whole planet, an entire ecosystem. We are deserts, droughts, floods and whirlwinds. We are sunlight, stardust and the dark of a bat-filled cave. We are rainbows and tornados. We are damp. We are lightning illuminating, empowered and in the next breath we turn to fog, clammy and confused. When life is moderate, dry and pleasant we seek adventure, when the thunder claps we cower indoors.

We want our ecosystem to cooperate, as if we were its maker. We are not: it is ours. Until we recognise that fact we will forever swim against the tide, getting pulled under by our own arrogance and presumption. We are part of something. We have no control. Or rather, we have some control, but we won't recognise it until we collide with our most natural self, with our truth, with our actuality.

What I learned today is simple: look not for sunshine, find the rain. When you find it, befriend it. For it is always bound to find you. Know that from here living grows. From the rain your soil is purged, your seed is burst. With rain we are washed free, released and, in time, made whole.

HARNESS THE POWER OF KING OF SWORDS

Capture those unexpected thoughts and feelings that you can barely hear your heart utter. Turn up the volume and assess what you are being told. Tune into your instinct, your intuition and leave the dial in place. Commit to the inner voice. Conclude not to be swayed by the influence, intention and voice of others.

DIRTY *&* DIVINE SPELLWORDS OF KING OF SWORDS

I am more than I am.

MY DIRTY & DIVINE
AFTERMATH

What if there is nothing else? What if there is no spirit? Those have been the questions dancing furtively around the edge of my mind as a result of completing this journey.

Just now I was putting my daughter to bed. I was singing to her. I was holding her hand. Her eyes were flickering and in the background I could hear birds singing. It was one of those moments I could have found deeply spiritual. Instead I found myself, not losing my faith, but questioning it,

When I started on a spiritual path I had guides and angels coming out of my arse. Signs were everywhere and everything. These days they are few and far apart. Life can get really hard and I don't see much miracle. Not really. This past tarot journey saw less than usual. It was intense, and I don't know what I am left with. I am left where I started, but my insides, my thoughts, have altered.

And so what of spirit? Is it a thing? Or not? Does it even matter?

Perhaps the very concept of nothingness is important. It keeps us on the edge of something more real. It is where I am at now. In a suburban village, getting real and being with each messy second. There are no archangels right now. There are no choirs of celestial guides descending upon me. I have no time for chanting or striking life-altering, soul-defying yoga poses. I take your kundalini and raise it with a kaleidoscope of grit, glitter paint and plastic.

Nothing particularly mystical has happened, except, perhaps, life itself.

I feel the touch of the flesh of my baby, of my daughter, of my husband so much better if I think there is a possibility that they are not real. That they will pass. That I will pass. That the beautiful gorgeous miracle of whatever this is, may not be here, may end. Maybe it is so true, because it is not, and yet, it maybe is... Perhaps that detail, life ever after, is not for me to behold at this time. The tarot have opened me directly to the moment. Nothing more. In this there is some magic. I have no time to stare at this potion, this conjuring. I will indulge it instead.

What happens next is that life continues. That which we set in motion will continue to unfold. For those of you with a curiosity for my tale, here is what happened next...

We got excited. Suddenly life blew open. My daughter's life flung us into the community. A dance show. Visits to the new school. A birthday party hosted from home, surrounded by friends and family. We went on holiday. We had a lovely time. This book got fully written. My husband got on top of his issues and things have been smoother. He has sought help from professionals and it is making things so much better. He is happier. I am happier. He said he wants another baby. He has come over all fatherly and it suits him. Some baby ducks were born in the village. Everyone stayed sniffle free (relatively). We got a trampoline. It is awesome. Baby started giggling, waving and experiencing herself. That is all.

As for me. I carried on with my creation, crafting this book, reading people's tarot, making myself useful and finding joy in it. I too had a health scare — apparently that theme is unending. I found some lumps on my cervix. The tests all came back clear. But in the meantime, I felt life crack open. And I realised, again, that we only ever have today. So I recommitted myself to life, to my power, to the things that I love.

As for my faith? Is it gone? It certainly isn't. I just perceive it more subtly now. It is in the way dust flies up and shimmers. It is there, somewhere, simmering away, unimportant and patient. I believe that a time for the divine will come. But right now, the dirt is where the party is at. So I scrape through life, floating and rustling, scheming and bustling. I create, I devise, I clean, I wish, I love, I live.

THE END OF YOUR JOURNEY

This isn't the end. This has been such a potent trip for me, and one that I feel would be worthwhile doing every few years. I hope you do too.

I believe that next time I do this, the results will be utterly different. That is the beauty of tarot, and indeed, of life. Tarot dig into your current reality and weed out that which is unhelpful. It is equally enlightening, painful, and, at times, it states the bloody obvious, which is where the magic works best: showing us what we already, deep down know. Then presenting new perspectives, giving us the right to be dirty and the permission to be divine.

So as you wrap up your path, your 78-day mission, what is it important to consider? Here is a little check list for you to work through, to ensure you amalgamate all the most important lessons and change.

PUT YOUR JOURNEY INTO WORDS

What words would you pluck out of the air to describe your journey? Choose five or six. Then whittle them down to two. Decide which represents your dirty, and which represents your divine. Then take those words with you into the future. Use them as your guiding light. Tattoo them on your wrist, write them in lipstick on your mirror. Trace them over your heart and keep them close to mind.

READ BACK

Read back through your journal. See how far you have come. Write any insights down as they come to you — new perspectives that you didn't perhaps have at the time. Channel them from your wisest self. Notice how it makes you feel. Do you feel like a different person? Do you feel silly at previous entries? Perhaps you see your own wisdom? Maybe you are surprised by your occasional insight, and your occasional lack of it. Comment on all this on a 'wrap up' page. Use this in the future as quick reminder.

SHUFFLE AND CUT

Shuffle your pack. Pick two cards. The first is Dirty. The second is Divine. With reverence and meditation and lit candles, gaze gently at them. Allow them to be the summary of all you have learned. Leave them out on a shelf for a week or so. Let their message be felt. Let it all be felt. Allow the learning to continue onward. It doesn't stop after 78 days. This is just the start.

BEYOND EXPECTATION

Make a mental note of what has dropped in and out of your journey. What did you think was important that got waylaid by life? What did you not expect to take over, that then became the story? I started my journey hoping for a career boost. What I got was the opposite, I got domestic drama and sickness. What did you hope for? What actually happened? Where did your hopes and expectation vanish, and what were they replaced with?

THE STORY NOT TOLD

Consider what hasn't been said, written or explored. I have several themes fizzling away in the back of my life that I haven't touched upon here. Not because I'm hiding them, but because, for the moment, they aren't for changing or challenging. They just are. Part of the stage setting, not yet pivotal or requiring deep examination, but there, waiting patiently for attention. These unspoken things are as much a part of this journey as anything that has been more brash, bold, brilliant and unbearable. Think on these things. Allow them some space to rise up and take centre stage. If they are on your radar, then it is likely they are next. . .

I know this journey has shaken me to the core. It didn't send outward change. It nudged and progressed inner change. Next time I do this I will find so much more about myself. Right now I have gleaned what I need for this moment. I am so glad I did it. I hope you are too. I didn't know if it would work. I didn't know who or what would come of all this. What came of it, was me.

THE END

The tarot are a plectrum with which a thousand notes can be strummed. They take you deeper than your prescribed self, further even than your divine feminine. They open a rainbow of self that abides in all that is. From the dirty and downtrodden to the sacred and succinct. The tarot reflect every prismatic shade, tone and colour your life might hold. They show you what you know, they show you what you have hidden from. Tarot only influence your life, in that they drag your attention towards what matters, and then, the tune changes. You make those changes, and spirit, divinity, orchestrates the whole deal. Cards being just one instrument, in a world filled with many.

The journey makes for a fuller version of you as it entangles you with the parts of yourself suppressed and oppressed by life thus far. It helps you navigate past the cultural boundaries and enter into a realm of archetype, deeper thought and archaic feeling. You embody them all, briefly, and herein you find aspects of yourself that were hidden long ago. Hidden by a society that limits us, to gender, to age, to title, to experience. You go beyond all of that. You move towards an understanding of yourself, your brittle, your brilliant, as all sacred. This journey isn't sacred; the cards are not sacred. You, and all that you do, and all that you learn from your escapades, that is where sacred lays.

In seeking yourself, you may have found everyone, everything. You are all. All is you. Boundaries melt away as we play with a pack of cards that ingeniously contains within it all that is divine, all that is dirty, and all that is in between. This has been a powerful tool of discovery. It has opened me to an expanded knowledge of my life. I found that this 'knowing' sat within, as it always was, covered only by the whims of a society that likes to place labels and keep us short and shallow. When indeed we are deep and long. All it required was for me to open and call.

This tarot journey has helped to clear the fog from my sights, for now. Though, in time, I will become shrouded again and further spiritual seekings will be sought to refresh my anxious self and blissed soul.

Those spiritual seekings always bring me back to my humanity, to my dirtiest, filthiest self. I suspect you will find the same. The learning, for me, is not in the prayer, or in the seeking of angels. It is in the tests, in the grunge, in the events I had rather not happened. Herein my Strength, my Star, my Empress and my loved Queen of Wands. They battle it out alongside me to try to become The Fool and The Chariot. They and I fight to join up all my dirt with the relieving balm that is just a little smidgen of divine.

In finding the divine, even just a passing scent of it, I am reminded, powerfully, that everything is unreal. The thoughts, opinions, events and judgements are all passing shades of nothing. They mean so little. Because of this I can trust in my innate powers, my soul's origin, my ever after. In abandoning the unreal, opening to the whiff of divinity and trusting in that which we cannot see, then our life becomes based on a more complex and readily available firmament: spirit, divinity, all that is real.

I am not a label or a man or a woman or even a human or a soul. I am infinite. I exist in the muck and melee and drama. I exist in the stars and hope and miracle. I, in human flesh, collaborate with my soul to conjure this life. And conjure it I do, with my thoughts, my faith, my desire and my fear. From here I can manifest a greater self, no longer shrouded by shackles, societal propaganda and self-loathing. I can become that which I always was. Sacred. And to think a little pack of cards was the prompt I needed. A little pack of cards and a dollop of effort, and here we are. Deeper than before. Open like never before. Allowing and allowed and ready for more. Let us be Dirty. Let us be Divine.

Welcome to your new reality, the forevermore of spirit, the freedom of divinity, the awe-invoking power of dirt, the sacred matter of your very being. Wow, welcome to that. Let this take your breath. And again I say it, and again I mean it, because there is nothing more to be said. Just, 'Welcome'. This is yours.

ABOUT THE AUTHOR

Alice Grist has 25 years' experience reading and teaching tarot. Certified in NLP, Hypnotherapy and Shamanism, Alice is a reiki master who has practiced spiritual healing since childhood.

Mother of two, and author of five books, *The High Heeled Guide to Spiritual Living* won Prediction Magazine's Best Book, and her work has garnered international acclaim as the perfect bridge for a modern reader to a more soulful life.

Alice is a frequent contributor to *Huffington Post, The Daily Love, Hello Giggles* and *The Conversation* writing about spirituality in her own quirky, accessible and fierce style.

OTHER BOOKS BY ALICE

The High Heeled Guide to Enlightenment (2009)

The High Heeled Guide to Spiritual Living (2011)

Dear Poppyseed, A Soulful Momma's Pregnancy Journal (2013)

Sinsational: Gritty Spirituality For Modern Women (2014)

Womancraft
PUBLISHING

Life-changing, paradigm-shifting books
by women, for women

Visit us at www.womancraftpublishing.com
where you can sign up to the mailing list and receive samples
of our forthcoming titles before anyone else.

(f)   Womancraft_Publishing

(y)   WomancraftBooks

(o)   Womancraft_Publishing

If you have enjoyed this book, please leave a review
on Amazon or Goodreads.

ALSO FROM WOMANCRAFT PUBLISHING

BURNING WOMAN

by Lucy H. Pearce

ISBN 978-1-910559-16-1

Burning Woman is a breath-taking and controversial woman's journey through history — personal and cultural — on a quest to find and free her own power.

Uncompromising and all-encompassing, Pearce uncovers the archetype of the Burning Women of days gone by — Joan of Arc and the witch trials, through to the way women are burned today in cyber bullying, acid attacks, shaming and burnout, fearlessly examining the roots of Feminine power — what it is, how it has been controlled, and why it needs to be unleashed on the world during our modern Burning Times.

Lucy H. Pearce's Burning Woman carries the torch of the sacred Feminine into the dark corners of women's unexpressed and unfulfilled desire and power. She dares us to burn down that which does not serve life, to use our fire to transform the world.

Oriah 'Mountain Dreamer' House

A must-read for all women! A life-changing book that fills the reader with a burning passion and desire for change.

Glennie Kindred, author of *Earth Wisdom*

by Lucy H. Pearce

ISBN 978-1-910559-06-2

A mazon bestseller in Menstruation. Hailed as 'life-changing' by women around the world, *Moon Time* shares a fully embodied understanding of the menstrual cycle. Full of practical insight, empowering resources, creative activities and passion, this book will put women back in touch with their body's wisdom. Whether the reader is coming off the pill, wanting to understand her fertility, struggling with PMS, healing from womb issues, coming back to cycles after childbirth or just wanting a deeper understanding of her body, *Moon Time* is an empowering read.

Lucy, your book is monumental. The wisdom in Moon Time sets a new course where we glimpse a future culture reshaped by honoring our womanhood journeys one woman at a time.

**ALisa Starkweather, author and founder of
the Red Tent Temple Movement**

LIBERATING MOTHERHOOD:
BIRTHING THE PURPLESTOCKINGS MOVEMENT

by Vanessa Olorenshaw

ISBN 978-1-910559-19-2

If it is true that there have been waves of feminism, then mothers' rights are the flotsam left behind on the ocean surface of patriarchy. Mothers are in bondage – and not in a 50 Shades way.

Liberating Motherhood discusses our bodies, our minds, our labour and our hearts, exploring issues from birth and breastfeeding to mental health, economics, politics, basic incomes and love and in doing so, broaches a conversation we've been avoiding for years: how do we value motherhood?

Highly acclaimed by leading parenting authors, academics and activists, with a foreword by Naomi Stadlen, founder of Mothers Talking and author of *What Mothers Do*, and *How Mothers Love*.

Lucid and riveting. . . This is The Female Eunuch of the 21st century.

Steve Biddulph, bestselling author of *Raising Boys, Raising Girls,* and *The Secret of Happy Children*

Liberating Motherhood is an important contribution to a vital debate of our times. Vanessa Olorenshaw speaks with warmth, wit and clarity, representing lives and voices unheard for too long.

Shami Chakrabarti, author of *On Liberty*, former director of Liberty and formerly 'the most dangerous woman in Britain'

THE OTHER SIDE OF THE RIVER:
STORIES OF WOMEN. WATER AND THE WORLD

by Eila Kundrie Carrico

ISBN 978-1-910559-18-5

A deep searching into the ways we become dammed and how we recover fluidity. This is a journey through memory and time, personal and shared landscapes to discover the source, the flow and the deltas of women and water.

Rooted in rivers, inspired by wetlands, sources and tributaries, this book weaves its path between the banks of memory and story, from Florida to Kyoto, storm-ravaged New Orleans to London, via San Francisco and Ghana. We navigate through flood and drought to confront the place of wildness in the age of technology.

Part memoir, part manifesto, part travelogue and part love letter to myth and ecology, *The Other Side of the River* is an intricately woven tale of finding your flow. . . and your roots.

An instant classic for the new paradigm.

Lucia Chiavola Birnbaum, award-winning author
and Professor Emeritus

THE HEROINES CLUB:
A MOTHER–DAUGHTER EMPOWERMENT CIRCLE

by Melia Keeton-Digby

ISBN 978-1-910559-14-7

Nourishing guidance and a creative approach for mothers and daughters, aged 7+, to learn and grow together through the study of women's history.

Each month focuses on a different heroine, featuring athletes, inventors, artists, and revolutionaries from around the world—including Frida Kahlo, Rosalind Franklin, Amelia Earhart, Anne Frank, Maya Angelou and Malala Yousafzai as strong role models for young girls to learn about, look up to, and be inspired by.

The Heroines Club is truly a must-have book for mothers who wish to foster a deeper connection with their daughters. As mothers, we are our daughter's first teacher, role model, and wise counsel. This book should be in every woman's hands, and passed down from generation to generation.

Wendy Cook, founder and facilitator of Mighty Girl Art

by Nicole Schwab

ISBN 978-1-910559-00-0

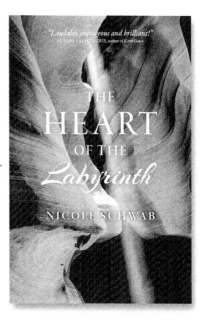

Reminiscent of Paulo Coelho's masterpiece *The Alchemist* and Lynn V. Andrew's acclaimed *Medicine Woman* series, *The Heart of the Labyrinth* is a beautifully evocative spiritual parable, filled with exotic landscapes and transformational soul lessons.

As everything she thought she knew about herself disintegrates: her health, career, family and identity, Maya embarks on a journey of discovery to the land of her ancestors. Coming face-to-face with her subconscious belief that being a woman is a threat, she understands that to step into wholeness she will have to reclaim the sacred feminine fire burning in her soul.

Once in a while, a book comes along that kindles the fire of our inner wisdom so profoundly, the words seem to leap off the page and go straight into our heart. If you read only one book this year, this is it.

Dean Ornish, M.D, President, Preventive Medicine Research Institute, Author of *The Spectrum*

MOODS OF MOTHERHOOD:
THE INNER JOURNEY OF MOTHERING

by Lucy H. Pearce

ISBN 978-1-910559-03-1

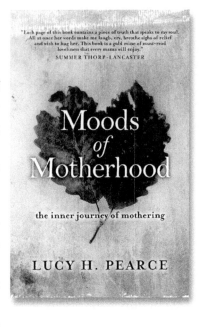

"Each page of this book contains a piece of truth that speaks to my soul. All at once her words make me laugh, cry, breathe sighs of relief and wish to hug her. This book is a gold mine of must-read loveliness that every mama will enjoy."

SUMMER THORP-LANCASTER

Moods of Motherhood charts the inner journey of motherhood, giving voice to the often nebulous, unspoken tumble of emotions that motherhood evokes: tenderness, frustration, joy, grief, anger, depression and love. Lucy H. Pearce explores the taboo subjects of maternal ambiguity, competitiveness, and the quest for perfection, offering support, acceptance, and hope to mothers everywhere. Though the story is hers, it could be yours.

This fully-updated second edition features 23 new pieces including posts written for her popular blog, *Dreaming Aloud*, her best-loved magazine columns and articles, and many other original pieces. This is a book full of Lucy's trademark searing honesty and raw emotions, which have brought a global following of mothers to her work.

Lucy's frank and forthright style paired with beautiful, haunting language and her talent for storytelling will have any parent nodding, crying and laughing along — appreciating the good and the bad, the hard and the soft, the light and the dark. A must-read for any new parent.

Zoe Foster, *JUNO* magazine

Printed in Great Britain
by Amazon

45460105R00158